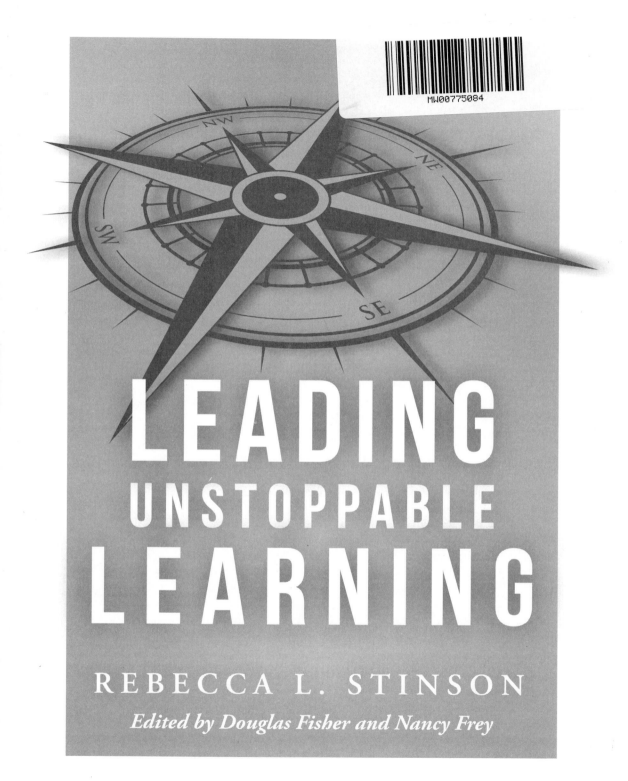

LEADING
UNSTOPPABLE
LEARNING

REBECCA L. STINSON

Edited by Douglas Fisher and Nancy Frey

Solution Tree | Press
a division of
Solution Tree

555 North Morton Street
Bloomington, IN 47404
800.733.6786 (toll free) / 812.336.7700
FAX: 812.336.7790

email: info@SolutionTree.com
SolutionTree.com

Visit **go.SolutionTree.com/leadership** to download the free reproducibles in this book.

Printed in the United States of America

21   20   19   18   17   1   2   3   4   5

Library of Congress Cataloging-in-Publication Data

Names: Stinson, Rebecca L., author. | Fisher, Douglas, 1965- editor. | Frey,
    Nancy, 1959- editor.
Title: Leading unstoppable learning / Author: Rebecca L. Stinson ; Editors:
    Douglas Fisher and Nancy Frey.
Description: Bloomington, IN : Solution Tree Press, 2017. | Includes
    bibliographical references and index.
Identifiers: LCCN 2016048518 | ISBN 9781943874255 (perfect bound)
Subjects: LCSH: Critical thinking--Study and teaching. | Reasoning--Study and
    teaching. | Learning strategies.
Classification: LCC LB1590.3 .S784 2017 | DDC 370.15/2--dc23 LC record available at https://lccn.loc
.gov/2016048518

Solution Tree

Jeffrey C. Jones, CEO
Edmund M. Ackerman, President

Solution Tree Press

President and Publisher: Douglas M. Rife
Editorial Director: Sarah Payne-Mills
Managing Production Editor: Caroline Weiss
Senior Production Editor: Tonya Maddox Cupp
Senior Editor: Amy Rubenstein
Copy Editor: Miranda Addonizio
Proofreader: Kendra Slayton
Text and Cover Designer: Rian Anderson
Editorial Assistants: Jessi Finn and Kendra Slayton

Acknowledgments

I cannot express enough thanks to the faculty at Claremont Academy. They push me to be smarter and to work harder; their unwavering commitment to collaboration for the students is undeniable. I offer my sincere appreciation to Mary Beth Padezanin, the assistant principal and my friend, the person who stands beside me. Because of her we have an exemplary instructional leadership team.

I could not have completed this project without the support of my friend and colleague, Robin Fogarty. She encouraged me with her kind words—thank you for allowing me to take time away from your writing project. The countless times you kept me on task will not be forgotten.

Finally, to my caring, loving, and supportive grandson, Marcus Anthony: my deepest appreciation. Your pushing of the keys on the computer when I had buried my head a little too long, the hand pull to the kitchen when it was time to eat, and the times when you just wanted Granny's attention kept me on schedule—your schedule. My heartfelt thanks.

Solution Tree Press would like to thank the following reviewers:

Taylor Barton
Principal
Lake Forest Elementary School
Sandy Springs, Georgia

Stephanie Ware
Principal
Oakdale Middle School
Ijamsville, Maryland

Carrie Porter
Assistant Principal
Northwestern Middle School
Milton, Georgia

Table of Contents

About the Editors

 **Douglas Fisher, PhD,** is professor of educational leadership at San Diego State University and a teacher leader at Health Sciences High and Middle College. He teaches courses in instructional improvement and formative assessment. As a classroom teacher, Fisher focuses on English language arts instruction. He was director of professional development for the City Heights Educational Collaborative and also taught English at Hoover High School.

Fisher received an International Reading Association Celebrate Literacy Award for his work on literacy leadership. For his work as codirector of the City Heights Professional Development Schools, Fisher received the Christa McAuliffe Award. He was corecipient of the Farmer Award for excellence in writing from the National Council of Teachers of English (NCTE) as well as the 2014 Exemplary Leader for the Conference on English Leadership, also from NCTE.

Fisher has written numerous articles on reading and literacy, differentiated instruction, and curriculum design. His books include *Teaching Students to Read Like Detectives, Checking for Understanding, Better Learning Through Structured Teaching,* and *Rigorous Reading.*

He earned a bachelor's degree in communication, a master's degree in public health, an executive master's degree in business, and a doctoral degree in multicultural education. Fisher completed postdoctoral study at the National Association of State Boards of Education focused on standards-based reforms.

Nancy Frey, PhD, is a professor of educational leadership at San Diego State University. She teaches courses on professional development, systems change, and instructional approaches for supporting students with diverse learning needs. Frey also teaches classes at Health Sciences High and Middle College in San Diego. She is a credentialed special educator, reading specialist, and administrator in California.

Before joining the university faculty, Frey was a public school teacher in Florida. She worked at the state level for the Florida Inclusion Network, helping districts design systems for supporting students with disabilities in general education classrooms.

She is the recipient of the 2008 Early Career Achievement Award from the Literacy Research Association and the Christa McAuliffe Award for excellence in teacher education from the American Association of State Colleges and Universities. She was corecipient of the Farmer Award for excellence in writing from the National Council of Teachers of English for the article "Using Graphic Novels, Anime, and the Internet in an Urban High School."

Frey is coauthor of *Text-Dependent Questions*, *Using Data to Focus Instructional Improvement*, and *Text Complexity: Raising Rigor in Reading*. She has written articles for *The Reading Teacher*, *Journal of Adolescent and Adult Literacy*, *English Journal*, *Voices in the Middle*, *Middle School Journal*, *Remedial and Special Education*, and *Educational Leadership*.

To book Douglas Fisher or Nancy Frey for professional development, contact pd@SolutionTree.com.

About the Author

 **Rebecca L. Stinson** is an administrator at Kingdom Schools in Riyadh, Saudi Arabia. She manages the teaching and learning around curriculum development, focusing specifically on planning, implementation, and evaluation. She is a mentor and a coach to over forty teachers from around the world. Rebecca is the former principal of Claremont Academy in the Chicago Public Schools (CPS) system, where she led for twelve years.

Rebecca has opened two new public schools and was recognized by the Illinois State Board of Education for achieving high scores in reading and mathematics, which put the schools in the top 7 percent of schools that were accelerating, or experiencing positive change, in student test scores. For this accomplishment, the CEO of CPS recognized Rebecca in the 2013 Principal Evaluations. That same year, she received the Principal Achievement Award for providing exceptional leadership for Chicago's students. Recognized as an imaginative professional developer, Rebecca has a passion for collaborating with her teachers to achieve success.

As president of The Stinson Group, Rebecca provides extensive trainings, professional development, and coaching sessions. Stinson is coauthor of *School Leader's Guide to the Common Core: Achieving Results Through Rigor and Relevance.* She is a past vice president of the Jack and Jill of America Chicago Chapter and a member of the Association for Supervision and Curriculum Development. She served as a member of the Office of Principal Preparation and Development as a mentor for new principals.

Rebecca has a bachelor of arts degree from Howard University in Washington, DC, and a master's degree in education from National Louis University in Chicago.

To book Rebecca L. Stinson for professional development, contact pd@Solution Tree.com.

Foreword

By Douglas Fisher and Nancy Frey

There's a leader in every seat. Think about it. Principals are not the only leaders in their schools and superintendents are not the only leaders in their districts. Everyone is, or could be, a leader. At its most basic level, leadership is about guiding the work of others. That certainly defines teachers who spend their days guiding the work of students. It would be so much easier if, instead of guiding, teachers just did all of the work for the students, right? But then learning wouldn't occur. Leaders and teachers must get others to engage in work. Hopefully that work is meaningful, because when it is, motivation, attention, and commitment increase.

But there's a leader in every seat. We must see students as leaders too. Through collaborative learning, as part of their work to consolidate their understanding, students guide the thinking and accomplishments of their peers. If they just sit around and fill out worksheets, they're probably not leaders. Instead, they're bored factory workers who have to replicate and repeat things over and over.

We could go on about the ways in which every member of a school can be a leader; instead, we'd like to focus our attention on the book in your hands. Following decades of research and teaching, we identified seven interrelated areas necessary for classrooms and schools to function effectively (Fisher & Frey, 2015). In our thinking, we divide the work of the teacher into these areas.

- Planning learning
- Launching learning
- Consolidating learning
- Assessing learning
- Adapting learning
- Managing learning
- Leading learning

These seven elements are in fact dependent on each other. A change to one will impact the others. Classrooms and schools operate as systems with connected parts. Imagine being the formal leader of a school or district in which you have provided teachers with excellent professional learning about adapting learning. They understand differentiation and accommodations. They know the difference among content, process, and product when it comes to the support they provide students. But if they are going to implement their knowledge, they should also know that changes in adapting learning will impact their planning, what they need to model as they launch learning, how they will assess learning, and how they will manage the learning environment. It's all connected.

But there's more, and we're so pleased that Rebecca Stinson was able to point this out. Formal leaders, such as principals, teacher leaders, curriculum coordinators, and superintendents, have to understand how each of these factors relates to their work. They have to lead teachers in revising the systems they use to improve students' learning. In this book, Rebecca Stinson shows how leaders can guide the thinking and work of teachers as they:

- Distinguish among the written, taught, and tested curricula
- Set learning targets with teachers
- Ensure rigor and support for all learners
- Use assessment information formatively
- Update grading policies
- Talk with parents about their children's progress
- Create a positive classroom climate

As Paul Manna (2015) notes, principals are multipliers of effective teaching. Principals have the ability to ensure that more and more students experience lessons that facilitate their growth and understanding. Principals can guide conversations about quality teaching and support teachers as they take risks to try new things. Yes, principals can magnify and multiply the best we all know how to do. Thankfully, this book shows us how. Rebecca Stinson is a leader of leaders guiding us through the process of making learning unstoppable for teachers and their students.

Introduction

*If your actions inspire others to dream more, learn
more, do more, and become more, you are a leader.*

—John Quincy Adams

When Rahm Emanuel was President Barack Obama's chief of staff, the two men shared a private joke. In response to the grueling, never-ending decisions they had to make each day, they decided, "One day they would open a T-shirt shack on a Hawaiian beach. And they would make no decisions about the inventory. The shirts would be in one color. And in one size" (Redford, 2014). When I heard this anecdote, I thought back to when I started as a building administrator—the first time I was exposed to the frequency and necessity of decision making as a leader.

When I first became a principal, I attended a required orientation. I was sitting at a table with veteran leaders and several neophytes. We were excitedly chattering away about all the good ideas we had and the difference we were going to make in our schools. I was listening a little more than I was talking because I wanted to hear what most people had to say. One woman in particular caught my attention. Even though I don't remember her name (she wasn't paired up as my mentor), I remember she had a deep, raspy voice and a strong presence. She was a seasoned principal with a warm smile and could tell I was listening intently. She turned to me and said that being a leader is all about making decisions—good decisions not about one classroom, one family, one teacher, or one student but about all of them. Every one of them.

In *Unstoppable Learning*, Douglas Fisher and Nancy Frey (2015) explain that leading is how administrators are able to create a vision and purpose for the work that teachers do, thereby developing a strong community and fostering growth in individuals and the organization. Quality leadership requires systems thinking. According to Fisher and Frey (2015), "*Systems thinking* is the ability to see the big picture, observe how the elements within a system influence one another, identify emerging patterns, and act on them in ways that fortify the structures within" (p. 2; emphasis added). No one can effectively lead without seeing the big picture. In my experience as a principal, I've learned that every single day, right after I say good morning, someone will ask me a question that requires me to make a decision or act on what I know. Those who intend to be systems thinking leaders must use these opportunities to make decisions that enable continual improvements to enhance student learning.

Unstoppable Learning's Good Leaders

Unstoppable Learning is a combination of two areas: good leadership and guiding principles. To facilitate it, good leaders must employ the following behaviors.

- Convey expectations.
- Learn about students (or teachers) and their goals.
- Provide background knowledge.
- Anticipate errors.
- Provide feedback and guidance.
- Conduct frequent check-ins.

Those behaviors link to the four principles of systems thinking (Fisher & Frey, 2015).

1. Relationships
2. Communication
3. Responsiveness
4. Sustainability

Relationships are stronger if leaders are familiar with their students and teachers. Communication is ineffectual if it doesn't convey expectations. Responsiveness leads to guidance and feedback. Leaders can create sustainability with the help of background knowledge and regular check-ins. In a systems thinking classroom, teachers use more than just the lesson to make decisions about student learning (Fisher & Frey, 2015). If a leader is to be a systems thinker, he or she must engage in all the behaviors of good leadership and utilize all four principles of systems thinking. Better conclusions and resolutions are reached not by using one behavior or by using one principle, but instead by using all in combination to leverage leadership.

That's who should read this book: new and established school leaders, superintendents who want to coach principals, principals who want to effectively lead teachers, and teacher leaders who manage colleagues. This book is even for teachers who are interested in knowing how to make sustainable changes in a school. School leaders are typically teachers who have progressed through additional education and training. But how does a new leader know if he or she is prepared for a leadership role? Good leadership behaviors can be researched, measured, and mimicked, but soft skills make the difference with implementation and sustainability. New leaders must ask themselves if they possess the soft skills necessary to achieve collaborative success—relationship building, civility, and integrity, for example (Colberg, 2016).

Unstoppable Learning (Fisher & Frey, 2015) discusses systems thinking within the classroom. *Leading Unstoppable Learning* extends these principles to the school and school leaders. It brings together the four principles of systems thinking with the elements of leading to answer the questions that drive leaders. None of the principles stand alone in this theory; instead, each overlaps with the others to create a mindset for successful decision making.

Relationships

Relationship building is a characteristic of good leaders, no matter the company or organization. According to Alan Colberg (2016), CEO of Fortune 500 company Assurant, "Technical skills are essential in helping [leaders] move forward in every career, but you also need to have strong 'soft' skills and one is relationship building." In *Unstoppable Learning*, Fisher and Frey (2015) talk about relationships in which interactions "change and develop every minute of the day and systems thinkers strive to respond to these fluctuations by monitoring the climate of the classroom and acting accordingly" (p. 3). True leaders in a school understand the need to foster relationships, modify plans, and respond to current needs. They should take time to learn about their teachers. Just like students, teachers arrive at school with different backgrounds and experiences. Only by building a relationship with each person can leaders achieve their potential. Leaders should ask themselves if all staff members have and are aware of a system of support—a system to provide professional development, materials, and guidance. As practitioners, teachers should be responsible for the learning in their classroom; after all, how teachers get their students to master the required standards is their field of expertise. As their leader, allow for errors but expect reflective practices. Require teachers to correct missteps. As part of relationship building, give meaningful guidance and feedback about instructional practices and having difficult conversations. Leaders should inform teachers that feedback sessions should result in classroom changes with evidence that leaders can see. By checking in with teachers frequently, leaders can show them that they care enough about them, their students, and their professional progression to follow up.

Finally, inspire teachers to become leaders by modeling leadership that nurtures all four systems thinking principles—relationships, communication, responsiveness, and sustainability.

Communication

Systems thinking communication creates lines of messaging to advance learning (Fisher & Frey, 2015). First, leaders must communicate to teachers their expectations of them. Teaching and learning will improve when teachers clearly understand what leaders expect. Leaders also communicate with all stakeholders and know the importance of that transfer of information—it increases buy-in and participation. Effective school leaders prioritize communication by distributing to all teachers and school staff a weekly message that explains what is going on in and around the school. Such memos are proactive (anticipating errors), informing staff of upcoming changes and events, rather than reactionary or after the fact. It is equally important to inform parents of such things and to encourage their involvement in school events and the school community. In *Parsing the Achievement Gap: Baselines for Tracking Progress,* Paul E. Barton (2003) cites parent or family involvement with the general community as a key to fostering higher education aspirations and more motivated students. Parent involvement in education promotes staff and student achievement because everyone works in tandem. But that tandem work doesn't occur without healthy communication (Barton, 2003). Communication with community members should also be a part of a school's fabric. This helps the school maintain relationships, especially those pertaining to gaining and renewing resources. In sum, having a regularly scheduled, proactive communication plan allows school leaders to build and maintain positive relationships with a variety of school stakeholders.

Responsiveness

Fisher and Frey (2015) assert that *responsiveness* requires an understanding that change occurs often, and that it is important to watch for and react to such changes. A responsive leader develops an inclusive environment and sets high expectations for staff members to establish pedagogical practices in the classroom that embrace diversity. He or she encourages reflection in his or her teachers to promote responsiveness. It is imperative for school leaders to display leadership that meets the diverse needs of social and cultural situations (Selznick, 1984). In addition to allowing for and adapting to the ever-changing social and cultural needs of a diverse school community, responsive leaders must also become a buffer for any negative situations that may arise within the school setting. Leaders must respond to everything that happens in the school building while also building bridges that focus on and support student and teacher achievement. It is important to be a supportive leader and inspire staff members to perform and expect the best.

Sustainability

Unstoppable Learning discusses sustainability through the lens of classroom teacher practices and illustrates how important it is to maintain, throughout the school, the habit of hard work established in the classroom (Fisher & Frey, 2015). Sustainable leadership reaches beyond and aims instead to create lasting, meaningful improvements in learning (Glickman, 2002; Stoll, Fink, & Earl, 2003). Schoolwide change can only happen when teachers believe the change improves their teaching, student achievement, and the school culture. This is the difference between doing something because you're told and doing something because you believe it will have an effect on the greater good. When implementing a change, a leader thinks about a whole-school improvement plan and how to ensure his or her leadership reaches throughout the building. Patchwork approaches aren't sustainable. Movement-of-the-moment is not something to latch on to. The implementation should result in a deep, far-reaching, and long-lasting change. Anticipating errors and communicating proactively go a long way toward increasing sustainability.

Implementing the Unstoppable Learning Model

Leading Unstoppable Learning brings together the four principles of systems thinking (relationships, communication, responsiveness, and sustainability) and good leadership behaviors (conveying expectations, learning about others, providing background, anticipating errors, providing feedback, and checking in frequently) and examines *Unstoppable Learning*'s critical elements as they pertain to leadership, the seventh element.

1. **Planning:** Focusing on learning's big picture

2. **Launching:** Challenging students to get past their misconceptions

3. **Consolidating:** Interacting with others to formalize knowledge

4. **Assessing:** Determining what's been learned versus taught

5. **Adapting:** Incorporating the assessment data and revising approaches

6. **Managing:** Cultivating and guiding the learning space

Each of these critical elements is the topic of a chapter in this book. Because Fisher and Frey structured *Unstoppable Learning* with questions, *Leading Unstoppable Learning* uses these questions to inform its leadership focus. The leadership that guides these elements depends on the good leadership behaviors listed earlier and highlighted in figure I.1 (page 6).

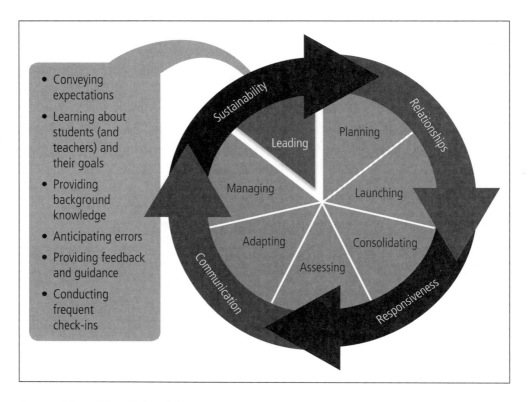

- Conveying expectations
- Learning about students (and teachers) and their goals
- Providing background knowledge
- Anticipating errors
- Providing feedback and guidance
- Conducting frequent check-ins

Sustainability · Relationships · Responsiveness · Communication

Leading · Planning · Managing · Launching · Adapting · Consolidating · Assessing

Source: Adapted from Fisher & Frey, 2015.

Figure I.1: Unstoppable Learning elements.

This Book as a Resource

If the goal of education is to create lifelong learners and curious students in a global society, then schools must have leaders who understand that they are not "fixing" students, but creating opportunities for students to learn in the best environment possible. Leaders are at the helms of educational institutions. Chapter 1, "Leading Learning Planning," focuses on leaders helping teachers plan purposefully. This chapter looks at learning's big picture and centers on how to lead the process of creating great classroom blueprints before the school year starts. It also looks at how leaders design a communication system that makes it clear what they expect of teachers. Chapter 2, "Leading Learning Target Launches," shows leaders what to expect when launching learning targets. It centers on how leaders put structures in place that enable teachers to transfer their lesson *planning* to actual *teaching*. This chapter also challenges teachers to get past their misconceptions. Chapter 3, "Leading Learning Consolidation," focuses on leaders examining student-centered classrooms with student-centered tasks. It helps leaders observe students using the information they've learned and see how students are interacting with others to formalize knowledge.

Chapter 4, "Leading Learning Assessment," recognizes the importance of measuring learning. This chapter guides leaders through monitoring formative assessment. It distinguishes between what is learned versus what has been taught by discerning lesson adjustment, coaching when providing feedback, and fine-tuning the teaching and learning processes. Chapter 5, "Leading Learning Adaptation," takes a deeper look into student needs through the lens of modifications, differentiation, and accommodations. Leaders must support and analyze data to revise approaches schoolwide. Chapter 6, "Leading Learning Management," emphasizes learning spaces. Leaders look at organizing learning beyond academics to create a focus for class and schoolwide expectations. Leaders make clear their high expectations from the beginning of the day with hospitable words and positive framing.

I suggest that leaders first read this book in its entirety. All its pieces work together to provide the skills that make a successful leader. However, I also recommend, within a network or collaborative leadership team, giving a good amount of attention to one chapter or focus area to implement. This dedicated focus will produce reflective thinking. Systems thinking leaders can support teachers by reviewing standards, talking with them about their unit plans, and offering feedback.

To think about the book in another way, consider George Posner and Alan Rudnitsky's (1986) assertion that any curriculum has at least five levels.

1. The *null* curriculum is what teachers do not teach.

2. The *hidden* curriculum is the culture's norms and values.

3. The *extra* curriculum is what teachers plan beyond the class.

4. The *operational* curriculum is what teachers teach and how they communicate it. This includes what the teacher instructs in class and the students' learning outcomes.

5. The *official*, or written, curriculum details basic lesson plans, including objectives and materials.

Chapters 1 and 2 focus on the last two—operational and official curricula—by addressing curriculum planning, learning targets, and knowledge consolidation. Chapter 3 straddles operational and extra curricula by addressing rigor and learning culture establishment at the classroom level. Chapter 4 focuses on the importance of the operational curriculum through the lens of assessment: How do leaders develop a balanced assessment plan to measure competency before instruction begins? Chapter 5 revisits operational and official curricula and reinforces a school's hidden curriculum by helping leaders communicate that all students deserve differentiation. Management topics and approaches in chapter 6 are another way to broach all five of Posner and Rudnitsky's (1986) curricula, most specifically the hidden curriculum—culture.

The beginning of each chapter reiterates *Unstoppable Learning's* driving questions for leaders. I recount anecdotes that reveal how I used each specific leadership element to make improvements in my school. Tools provide guidance for readers' own leadership. Each chapter contains a discussion linking the leadership element to systems thinking and simple forms that create structure, set expectations, and facilitate a systematic way of collecting information. The chapters end with driving questions designed to get leaders, networks, and school teams thinking about what current systems will help them achieve the changes they desire at their schools.

Hopes for Readers

When I started this writing journey, I was the principal of Claremont Academy in Chicago, Illinois—a place I had been for twelve years. While writing this book, I moved into a new administrative role at an international school in Riyadh, Saudi Arabia. In my new role, I found that I needed one place where I could find a resource for leading. My hope is that readers who are in the work of leading select *Leading Unstoppable Learning* as a resource for systems thinkers—those who know that student achievement depends on all elements working together. May this book be your one place.

The forms used throughout the book are designed to bring value to the leadership experience. They are simple in nature because the focus is on the work and coaching that follow. The advantages to using simplistic documents are threefold: (1) it creates structure, (2) it sets expectations, and (3) it facilitates systematic data collection. Every school and every leader has different needs, but the big question is the same: As a leader, how do I systemically support and coach teachers for improved teaching and learning?

CHAPTER 1

LEADING LEARNING PLANNING

Four steps to achievement: Plan purposefully. Prepare prayerfully. Proceed positively. Pursue persistently.

—William Arthur Ward

I remember a time when purposeful planning's importance was very clear: I was observing a first-grade teacher who was introducing students to the week's new sight words. Most students did not know the words, but five did. They recognized them from the pretest. When I saw this, I asked myself what those five students were learning. How many minutes of daily instruction did the teacher dedicate to words or work they already knew? Wouldn't they (and the remaining students) benefit more if the teacher had planned differentiated instruction before the day began?

Because systems thinking leaders help guide teachers, purposeful planning is one of the most important aspects of the role. *Unstoppable Learning* (Fisher & Frey, 2015) recommends that leaders begin a planning process by considering these driving questions:

- Do the teachers know their students?
- Are the teachers' efforts consistent with school improvement efforts?
- How does the teacher's unit of instruction relate to the annual goals for students?
- Does the teacher have the tools necessary to teach this content?
- What is the teacher's plan to collect evidence of student learning?

- What are the teacher's next steps?
- How do we communicate the school's high expectations to students, faculty, and parents? (p. 173)

Start by asking yourself these questions as you work through the sections in this chapter on planning curriculum and communication.

When they help teachers create unit instruction, leaders put into action all the systems thinking principles—relationships, communication, responsiveness, and sustainability. They also exhibit good leadership by guiding unit instruction creation, ensuring teachers have the necessary tools, and planning communication. Engaging with teachers to develop courses that focus on expectations and student growth *before* the academic year begins helps ensure every grade level has coherent instruction.

Guiding Unit Instruction Creation

Planning helps teachers organize their thinking, prepare for group instruction, and stay on trajectory. Leaders should monitor planning, and they should monitor instruction. When they are reviewing written plans, leaders should look at instruction simultaneously.

The time to start thinking of and researching fun ideas is when leaders plan curriculum with teachers before the school year. But this requires responsiveness, too. Systems thinking leaders can't expect teachers to follow curriculum verbatim; everyone must adjust to students and meet them where they are. Leaders help guide the creation of the official and operational curricula.

Official Curriculum

Teachers are responsible for teaching the official curriculum—the state or national standards—every school year. Leading a school in systems thinking means helping teachers broadly assess their official curriculum and begin to develop the operational curriculum. Purposeful planning means a thorough official curriculum; educators cannot do this work on the fly. Systems thinking requires that leaders convey their curricular expectations and guide teachers to that end.

Help teachers unpack standards into a proper scope and sequence to give them a year's worth of outcomes in two concise statements. According to the Board of Studies, Teaching and Educational Standards NSW (BOSTES), "Scope and sequence is an important step in the design of effective teaching and learning programs for a course. [Scope] summarizes what is to be taught and the sequence in which it will be taught" (p. 6). For example, figure 1.1 shows the scope and sequence that a Chicago school adopted based on the Common Core State Standards (National Governors Association Center for Best Practices [NGA] & Council of Chief State School Officers [CCSSO], 2010). The sequence followed the learning targets as they appear in figure 1.1.

English Language Arts Common Core State Standards					
Grade 2 Scope and Sequence					
X—Not taught					
I—Introduced					
T—Teaching to proficiency (Assessed)					
R—Reinforced		**Quarter**			
CCSS: Reading—Literature (Scope)	**Long-Term Learning Targets**	**1**	**2**	**3**	**4**
RL.2.1. Ask and answer such questions as who, what, where, when, why, and how to demonstrate understanding of key details in a text.	Students will be able to ask questions before, during, and after reading to help them understand the meaning of a literary text. (For example, who, what, where, when, why, and how.) Students will be able to answer questions during and after reading to show their understanding of a literary text. (For example, What did you learn from this story?)	T	T	T	T
RL.2.2. Recount stories, including fables and folktales, from diverse cultures and determine their central message, lesson, or moral.	Students will be able to recount and retell a story using important details. (For example, Recount the text justifying the message.) Students will be able to determine the important message, lesson, or moral in a story. (For example, What is the central message, lesson, or moral in the text?)	I	T	R	X
RL.2.3. Describe how characters in a story respond to major events and challenges.	Students will be able to describe how characters in a story solve problems and overcome challenges. (For example, How does the character respond to the major event in the story?)	X	I	T	T
RL.2.4. Describe how words and phrases (for example, regular beats, alliteration, rhymes, repeated lines) supply rhythm and meaning in a story, poem, or song.	Students will be able to describe how rhymes, repeated lines, and alliteration supply rhythm and meaning in songs and poems. (For example, What is the tone of the text?)	I	I	T	T

Sources: Claremont Academy, 2015; NGA & CCSSO, 2010.

Figure 1.1: Scope and sequence example based on CCSS.

Once they have fleshed out the scope, teachers must then think through when they will introduce, teach, assess, and reinforce each standard—the sequence. Systems thinking leaders facilitate purposeful planning by looking at each teacher's planned scope and sequence and identifying whether they have scheduled all the standards for the school year. Flexibility is required. A curriculum isn't written in stone, of course, but advise teachers against planning only a week in advance with the aid of fun online activities. Online ad hoc lessons can appeal to time-poor teachers, but many of those lessons do not align with standards.

Deeper reflection on standards shows that purposeful planning reinforces interconnections—across and between subjects. For example, during a Thinking Core workshop in Chicago, Illinois, Diana Dumetz Carry explained how, using a complex text, students can demonstrate an author's theme and provide a summary using textual evidence. She also began to make the anchor standards connection. Standards tend to build on themselves, which requires carrying a thread throughout most of, if not an entire, academic year. That, in turn, requires careful planning. Lead teachers to that approach by stressing its importance and supporting their efforts. The first step in this process is for teachers to learn the standards they are required to teach. It is important to know the end-of-year student expectations. The second step is for teachers to determine when they will introduce, teach, and assess each standard. These same standards are built into *all* lessons. After planning the official curriculum, teachers have a focus for the entire school year. I examine how teachers can plan for what they actually teach in the following section on operational curriculum.

Operational Curriculum

While the official curriculum is usually district or state mandated, the operational curriculum, at the school level, requires leadership so students successfully achieve the standards. Systems thinking requires leaders to develop the school year's focus sequentially, connecting the standards, the unit plan, and the weekly lesson plan. This linear planning format helps teachers stay aligned throughout the year, moving from the standards plan (scope and sequence) to the plan by term (unit plan) to the plan by week (lesson plan).

Unit Plans

Systems thinking requires teachers to draw their unit plans directly from their long-term goals or the official scope and sequence. Systems thinking leaders can support teachers by reviewing the standards and unit content, conversing with teachers about their unit plans, and offering feedback.

Leaders and teachers can effectively examine unit plans via the backward design model (Wiggins & McTighe, 2005). Examining unit plans by the model's three stages can help leaders intercept errors and revise during planning before students begin the class (Wiggins & McTighe, 2005).

1. Know what the goal is. The standards determine the learning targets.

2. Decide what it looks like when students meet goals.

3. Plan unit instruction.

Monitor unit plans to ensure alignment to scope and sequence. Figure 1.2 is a sample rubric that systems thinking leaders can give to teachers to self-assess their unit plans. It clearly identifies the guidelines for what leaders require of teachers to link their individual classes and unit plans to the wider school and its goals for student learning. Leaders will see improvement in the quality of work they receive when teachers clearly understand what leaders expect of them.

Unit	
Standards **Scope and sequence**	☐ Identify major focus standards. ☐ Sequence standards according to scope and sequence.
Assessments	☐ Create preassessments. ☐ Create formative assessments. ☐ Include progress monitoring. ☐ Align assessments to standards. ☐ Include research simulation (comparison of two or more texts with similar themes). ☐ Create summative assessments.
Field experience	☐ Identify field experience (student trip, guest speaker, opportunity to consolidate learning). ☐ Relate activity or assessment to learning expectations.
Technology integration	☐ Support instruction and learning with technology. (Computer skill builders are not technology integration.) ☐ Relate activity or assessment to learning expectations.
Arts integration	☐ Identify arts integration to consolidate learning. ☐ Relate activity or assessment to learning expectations.
Texts and materials	☐ Include rigorous texts. ☐ Include various representations of concepts. ☐ Include a mix of literature and informational texts.
Weekly plans in unit	☐ Scaffold instruction. ☐ Identify differentiation.

Source: Claremont Academy, 2015.

Figure 1.2: Teacher unit-plan review—self-assessment.

*Visit **go.SolutionTree.com/leadership** for a free reproducible version of this figure.*

In addition to conducting initial planning meetings and providing rubrics or checklists to enable teachers to self-assess their unit plans, systems thinking leaders should encourage their teachers to reflect on their practice. Leaders must incorporate opportunities for teachers to write about their units when they are done teaching. Figure 1.3 guides teachers in their reflection.

Teacher Reflection on Unit Plan

Unit: _____

Date taught: _____

What did I like about the unit? _____

What will I do differently next time? _____

Did my students master the standards? _____

What evidence proves that? _____

What can I take to my teacher team? _____

What can I take to my principal? _____

Figure 1.3: Teacher reflection on unit plan.

*Visit **go.SolutionTree.com/leadership** for a free reproducible version of this figure.*

Systems thinking requires that teachers think globally, and reflection helps them by improving their collaboration and communication, which helps lead to Unstoppable Learning.

Lesson Plans

The operational curriculum planning road does not end at the unit plan. Teachers are also responsible for creating weekly lesson plans that drill down into more detail. There are numerous lesson plan designs (for examples, see Fisher & Frey, 2014). What is important is that school leaders take the time to review the plan.

Leaders use a variety of techniques when reviewing weekly lesson plans. Some ask for all teachers to email the weekly lesson plans before the first day of the week. Others ask teachers to put lesson plans in the assistant principal's mailbox. To review the weekly lesson plan in person, sit in the classroom and analyze the plan with the teacher. This method provides time for an impromptu visit, which helps build relationships.

Avoid getting bogged down looking at too many components of too many lesson plans in one day, all while trying to give actionable feedback. The number of plans a person can look at daily depends on the school population and support system. Focus on two aspects of the lesson plan every week to keep learning at the teaching level sustainable over time. For example, during the first month of school, a leader may examine the scope and sequence aspects of the lesson plans to make sure that teachers have vertically aligned their plans from the scope and sequence to the unit plan to the lesson plan. Ensure that the standards are in the scope and sequence and that they're addressed in the unit plan and lesson plan. As the weeks progress, continue adding to the review. Figure 1.4 is an example of a finished progressive review school leaders can conduct for lesson plans.

Teacher: _Ms. Kim Lovetoteach_

Unit plan: _In My Neighborhood_

Standards aligned with scope and sequence?: _Scope and sequence aligned; five-week unit_

Instructional design or lesson plan date: _September 7_

Standard: _Focus standards accurately noted. The fact that you don't have Reading standard 1 standing alone is fantastic—you have it paired with another standard._

Differentiation evidence: _It seems you have differentiation only one time per week. How are you able to reach all of your students?_

Figure 1.4: Weekly lesson-plan review for leaders.

*Visit **go.SolutionTree.com/leadership** for a free reproducible version of this figure.*

The operational curriculum is very teacher focused in terms of planning and very student focused in terms of learning. The school leader's goal is to ensure the teaching and learning are focused on the standards and that evidence is collected to show intended growth.

Ensuring Teachers Have the Necessary Tools

At the same time that leaders help teachers create and fine-tune unit plans and weekly lesson plans, they should assess whether teachers have the necessary tools—novels, dry-erase markers, paper, and technology, for example. Because they attend fundraisers, work under district guidance, and interact with legislators—sometimes directly, sometimes indirectly—leaders bear extra weight where this topic is concerned. Leaders can't help teachers get what they need without being responsive. Teachers can write grants (or use websites such as www.DonorsChoose.org) to increase or improve classroom resources.

Planning Communication

Since leaders themselves do not teach in classrooms, they must communicate with others to influence their behavior. Plan on making the message clear, at regular intervals, to all stakeholders—staff, students, and parents.

With Staff

The principal must communicate goals to staff members to help instill the desire to perform at a high level (English, 2008). There are several methods to communicate with staff and faculty members. Communicating weekly with teachers through email keeps everyone well informed. I used a weekly email bulletin as a building leader, and it conveyed my expectations for teachers, provided clear directions and guidance for how to meet these expectations, and enabled open electronic communication among teachers about what was going on in school. Instead of printing it, I emailed the bulletin and placed an electronic copy on a shared staff drive before the first day of the work week. It contained information on the upcoming week, updates for all school leaders and committees, and messages from the dean or the climate coach. This communication eliminated the need for multiple memos throughout the week from different groups. Instead, these groups simply emailed their announcements to the school leader at the end of each week; in turn he or she submitted that information to me for bulletin inclusion. The sample bulletin in figure 1.5 shows these principles of open communication.

The Week at a Glance

Monday, January 4	First day of class
Tuesday, January 5	Team meeting (3:30 p.m.) and gradebook check
Wednesday, January 6	Mathematics grade-level meetings
Thursday, January 7	Don't forget to do your positive logs!
Friday, January 8	Progress reports distributed

"Don't worry when you are not recognized, but strive to be worthy of recognition." —Abraham Lincoln

Administration

Priorities:

1. Differentiation based on data
2. Climate and culture (social and emotional learning)
3. Professional development
   - The expectation of the gradebook is to show **student mastery of standards**. Is this evident in yours?

- There should be consistency of standards—a focus standard—evident through classwork, formative assessment, and summative assessment that shows progression, growth, and mastery. If students aren't mastering the standards, what is your plan to revisit the assessment or assignment?

- A multitiered system of support (MTSS) red folder MUST be started for any student who is off track or not meeting standards.

- Do students have an opportunity to redo the assignment or assessment? This should be evident in the retake section of the gradebook.

- Look at the expectations of the gradebook and make sure you are meeting them.

- You should preplan assessments with your units and pre-enter them in your gradebook as your road map for instruction and mastery.

- **Progress reports** are distributed on Friday. Students must have grades entered in every subject.

Finger on the pulse of your class: Do you know where your students are? We are finishing week fifteen. How many of your students are off track? Are you reviewing data to help you group students? If you don't continually use your data (your gradebook and assessments as well as PM [progress monitoring] and NWEA [Northwest Evaluation Association] or MAP [Measures of Academic Progress] testing) you won't get the student growth you expect. Differentiation is key. Teaching the same thing, the same way, with the same expectation will not work. Really get to know your students and their needs and where they fit overall in your class.

Subjects

Mastery: How do you know which of your students have mastered each of the Common Core State Standards for your grade level?

Purpose: Do your lessons have purpose? Do the students know why they are learning each concept, and can they articulate this to a visitor in your classroom?

Grade-Level Meetings

Meetings will take place on Wednesday during your prep period with the exception of one teacher: Ms. Strange, Wednesday at 8:15 a.m. We will review your binders during your grade-level meetings this week. During our last meeting we reviewed NWEA data. Please come to the meeting prepared to discuss the students you have identified to reach 50 percent or higher and what your plan of instruction is to ensure the success of these students.

Counselor

Congratulations. We are entering the year with 96 percent attendance.

Call the homes of all students absent Monday, January 4, 2016. Log all calls in student logger under attendance.

Keep all attendance books up to date; each book should have all documents in each section.

Source: Claremont Academy, 2015.

Figure 1.5: Weekly electronic bulletin to communicate with staff.   continued →

Social and Emotional Learning Committee and Climate Coach

Social and emotional learning (SEL): The start of a new year is a natural time to reestablish the operation of your classroom. It is a great time to set goals for your students and hold them accountable. Take the first day or two back to review expectations, talk with your students about goals and positive mindsets, practice routines, and set high expectations. Hold circles (all-class group time) to find out how they spent their vacation break (shows you are interested in them) and share with them what you did on your break (reminds them that you are actually a person). Hold a circle to plan how you will operate this year and review NWEA scores, grades, and gather ideas from students about how to best approach their academics (shows them how to set measurable goals). If you need ideas, please check the SEL folder in Drive, research "community building activities," or email me!

Schoolwide expectations (hallway supervision):

- Remember that every student should have a pass to be in the hallway.
- Adults who are traveling through the building with students should be at the rear of the line. Your line leaders should be trusted students who know the stopping points in the hallway.

Quick wins:

- Praise or acknowledge your (and other) students for behaving appropriately, especially in the hallway.
- Remind all colleagues about schoolwide expectations. We all are capable of helping each other out!

Health Tips From the Healthy Schools Committee

With the new year comes the opportunity for a fresh start. For many people, this means leading a healthier lifestyle. If this is your goal, follow these tips to stay on track. What is motivating you to eat better and be more active? Do you want to look better in your clothes, feel more energetic, or simply improve your health? Check back for our New Year, New You tips.

With Parents and Students

Communicating once weekly over the phone (leaving texts or voice mails) about school highlights helps parents and students stay apprised of what's happening. A biweekly or monthly newsletter similar to the one for faculty can help you send a sustainable message. Your school's parent-teacher organization or communications manager may be in charge of the entire newsletter, with the principal responsible for an article or essay and general oversight.

Asking Driving Questions for Planning Learning

Planning is crucial because it ensures a realistic, sustainable proposal for monitoring and evaluating implemented changes; planning sets the school's direction. It is through this framework—akin to the standards in the classroom—that a school organizes itself, examines its established goals, and makes adjustments. It is the leader's job to work with all stakeholders in an environment that encourages shared decision making with student learning at the forefront.

Planning purposefully means that systems thinking leaders must forecast how to reach goals and regularly communicate this information to students, teachers, and other stakeholders. That communication includes topics like how to unpack standards and tailor instruction to reflect those learning targets. Effective communication means leaders need to get to know teachers more deeply so they can be sure to pass on the guidance, feedback, and professional support teachers need. Systems thinking, as Fisher and Frey (2015) explain in *Unstoppable Learning*, asks that leaders plan purposefully for this communication. When they execute these plans, they help teachers plan for the school year, all while modeling best practices.

A systems thinking leader must consider the following five driving questions concerning purposeful planning.

1. Are the school's priorities and focus for the year based on standards? How often should I check in so I can see trends?

2. How can I learn about my teachers' strengths and provide the resources and professional development they need to be successful?

3. How will I monitor schoolwide goal achievement?

4. How will I know if teachers are taking the information from professional development to the classroom?

5. In what form will I communicate important information, expectations, and feedback? How often and to what audiences?

CHAPTER 2

LEADING LEARNING TARGET LAUNCHES

*The man who can make hard things
easy is the educator.*

—Ralph Waldo Emerson

At Claremont Academy, the school year started off with leaders engaging teachers in pedagogy sessions to highlight the importance of students knowing the intent of every lesson. Teachers read articles, watched videos, and discussed the importance of students knowing what they were learning. On the first day of school, I walked into every classroom to see if the teachers had posted learning targets. Of the twenty-five classrooms I visited, twenty-three had learning targets clearly visible—a promising outcome. I posted a statement of congratulations in the schoolwide bulletin and held personal coaching conversations with the teachers who were not in compliance with the goal.

That was the good news. My subsequent classroom visits did, however, help me identify some learning target implementation weaknesses. Firstly, several teachers hadn't collected learning evidence. Students needed learning targets that were more explicitly written. I knew this because during the classroom visits, I asked students questions such as, "What are you working on?" and "What are you learning right now?" Instead of answers that aligned with learning targets—"We're learning how to summarize stories" and "We're multiplying fractions"—students gave answers like, "We have to write sentences from the story" and "We're doing math."

Learning targets should focus on not only what teachers expect students to do but what they expect students to learn. A teacher's success with students hinges on his or her ability to launch learning targets. A *learning target* is not only what students will learn but how deeply they'll delve and how they will show what they learned (Moss & Brookhart, 2009).

In *Unstoppable Learning*, Fisher and Frey (2015) set the stage for formal leaders with these driving questions:

- Are the teachers' expectations for students grade-level appropriate?
- How do [principals and teachers] communicate these expectations to students?
- Have [principals and teachers] made these expectations relevant to students?
- Does the teacher know what misconceptions and errors to anticipate?
- How will the teacher hook students?
- What are the teacher's next steps? (p. 174)

As with curricular planning, leaders are best leading learning target launches when they encourage teachers to reflect on their own expectations and define learning targets.

Encouraging Teachers to Reflect on Their Expectations

Communicating with teachers honestly about their expectations for students is important. If their expectations don't align with the given standards, which should in turn align with student ability, they must address the resulting gap. Sometimes it can be tough for a teacher, someone who works so closely with students every day, to see this objectively.

The best teaching requires reflection, and systems thinking leaders are responsible for assisting teachers in this process. The teacher unit-plan review self-assessment in figure 1.2 (page 13) helps leaders give teachers a reflection starting point. Focusing on units and students can be easier than focusing on oneself.

A simple reflection tool can help teachers move to launching learning targets. During a coaching session, I have teachers identify students they believe are below, at, and above grade-level expectations. I record those names for the purpose of inter-viewing students during classroom visits. The goal of the visit is to see if all students know what is expected of them during the lesson. Teacher reflection should be based on what we actually do—not on what we *think* we are doing. Visit **go.SolutionTree .com/leadership** to access a free reproducible teacher reflection form.

Leaders must collect qualitative data from teachers with the intent of taking the next step—implementing an action to improve or streamline. They should ensure that teachers know that taking action is part of the process and that it benefits students as well as the teachers themselves. This will help avoid the too-common attitude of, "I'm doing this because my principal told me to" and shift thinking to, "I'm doing this because my students are benefiting."

Defining Learning Targets as a Leader

Systems leaders can ensure that teachers infuse their lessons with purpose. Encourage and remind teachers to state the overall learning target—what students should take away from the lesson—at the beginning *and* end of the lesson. One teacher explained:

> The lesson [allowed] plenty of time for me to assess during instruction, but I didn't. I just kept going. Reflecting on these shortcomings has provided me with many ideas on how to improve. The most important change has been the purposing of the lesson. While I still follow the template, I make sure I tell students why being able to do the standard is an important part of reading and writing. (Tammara Wofford, personal communication, November 2015)

Leaders define and monitor evidence of learning standards by focusing on the big picture—what they expect students to learn. In addition to assessing learning targets with walkthroughs, casual student interviews, and data monitoring, leaders can help teachers via peer observations. Encouraging teachers to help students see the relevance and relatedness of the learning targets helps as well. Finally, leaders must communicate with students about learning targets.

Peer Observations

The Claremont Academy collaborative team developed a four-question peer-observation form (see figure 2.1, page 24) to sustain teacher development around learning targets. Teachers visited each other's classes. Peers recorded their observations on the checklist, which the principals in turn shared with the teacher at a follow-up debriefing. Teachers shared with each other to help teachers feel safe giving honest feedback. Peer observations were not part of the formal observation process.

The teacher in the following example articulated the learning target—she clearly told the students. However, when leaders asked, "What are you doing today? Do you know why this is important?" the students couldn't explain. She did not accomplish the goal.

Question	Yes or No	Evidence
Does the teacher state the standards-based learning objective in words or in writing?	Yes	Teacher says: "Today we are going to read Ruby Bridges, and we are going to look at what the characters say in each paragraph to figure out the author's message." This is the standard that asks students to know how characters respond. Standard not on the board.
Has the teacher selected complex text?	Yes	The text is Lexile ranked for this grade.
Does the teacher identify the standard?	Yes	Teacher says: "The standard is how characters respond."
Do students articulate what they are doing and why it is relevant to their learning?	No	Student 1 says: We are going to read today. Student 2 says: Ruby Bridges?

Figure 2.1: Teacher peer-observation form.

Visit go.SolutionTree.com/leadership for a free reproducible version of this figure.

Providing peer observation is always a win. Receiving and giving this kind of feedback allows teachers to recognize and rectify their errors. Remember, systems thinking leadership is about motivating people to reflect on their practice and make changes.

Relevance and Relatedness

We have all heard students wonder why they "need to know this" and what a learning target "has to do with my life." When leaders help teachers launch learning targets, they should make sure teachers relay relevance to their students. Per Roberson (2013), "Relevance is important to teaching and learning because it is directly related to student engagement and motivation." Students do not see relevance on the whiteboard. Teachers must make the relevance clear. Relevance is so significant that as a leader, I also ask students why their learning is important. When leaders require relevance, they will know teachers are asking themselves the following student driving questions about learning targets from *Unstoppable Learning*:

- What do I already know?
- What will I learn?
- Why will I learn it? (Fisher & Frey, 2015, p. 174)

Relatedness is another tool leaders can use when coaching teachers about relevance. Per Roberson (2013), "Relatedness is an inherent need students have to feel close to the significant people in their lives, including teachers." Students often go home and say they did nothing—"School was fine"—because they view much of what they learn as unimportant or irrelevant to themselves. Help teachers understand the imperative to make information relevant and relatable. Student achievement is the result. Studies show that motivation is higher in students whose teachers relate to them and show them how the content relates to them (Ryan & Deci, 2000).

I encourage teachers to start the year off by telling students their own stories. It can be anything from an interesting anecdote about their lives to how they decided to become a teacher—so long as it breaks the ice and initiates relatedness. Throughout the year I reiterate to teachers that they can use themselves as examples in their writing. For example, if students know the teacher likes basketball, she can write word problems that show her dribbling multiple basketballs. While this is not required, I highly encourage it because it leads to targeted learning. Leaders can help teachers find relevance and relatedness with themselves as well—relationships being one of the four systems thinking principles, of course—with this same approach. Leaders can tell teachers *their* stories.

Communication With Students About Learning Targets

Leaders must know how to communicate with students to assess whether they know their learning targets. They should hear student chatter about the learning targets before and during the lesson. Students can use dialogue to make sense of the information the teacher presents.

The first question leaders should ask students when they walk into a classroom is, "What are you working on?" At this point, leaders should look for students to begin with the unit, the text, or the essential question, and to move right into the standard or learning target. Students can sit through hours of instruction and not know where they are going or what teachers will expect of them. Leaders don't want that. After asking about the learning target, I immediately follow up with, "Do you know why this is important?"

Asking Driving Questions for Launching Learning Targets

A leader understands the importance of everyone in the classroom knowing the learning target and its relevance. Students should never spend a moment guessing or wondering what they are doing or why.

A systems thinking leader must consider these five driving questions about launching learning targets.

1. Do I, as the leader, understand learning targets?

2. Have I trained my teachers to understand how to write and communicate learning targets?

3. Can I observe students articulating the standard they are practicing and understanding why they are learning it (not just reciting it)? Do students know when they are successful?

4. Are students connecting the standard to relevance and why it is worth learning?

5. If the process isn't seamless, what can I do as the leader to create opportunities for growth? What corrective measures might we take?

CHAPTER 3

LEADING LEARNING CONSOLIDATION

The function of education is to teach one to think intensively and to think critically. Intelligence plus character—that is the goal of true education.

—Martin Luther King Jr.

During a second-grade classroom visit, I noticed the teacher was leading his students through a sight-word lesson. Many students already knew the words. The lesson's complexity wasn't enough to challenge those students. After I initiated some reflection, the teacher researched and decided that next time he would follow up with a leveled partner reading activity. The students who were ready to move on could select a book from the classroom library to read to each other. The increased student-to-student interaction facilitated learning consolidation. Students could thus practice additional skills: student choice and collaboration. I observed a remarkable transformation during the next lesson. The students who knew their sight words moved forward to consolidate their learning through reading books that contained the words and the teacher wasted no valuable instructional time.

When students consolidate their learning, they move from *what* they learned to *how* they use the information they learned. Lesson complexity is vitally important when learning consolidation is the goal.

Fisher and Frey (2015) suggest the following driving questions in *Unstoppable Learning* to encourage leaders' systems thinking about consolidating learning:

- Are students using academic language on a regular basis?
- What did the students' demonstration of learning say about the lesson?
- Did the evidence of learning match the teacher's expectations?
- How are students gaining independence? (p. 175)

Leading learning consolidation asks responsiveness and communication of leaders. Guidance, feedback, and frequent progress checks help reinforce the systems thinking approach in the classroom, and the school at large, so learning moves to *how*—consolidation. Establishing a culture of learning independence helps students consolidate their learning.

Establishing a Culture of Learning Independence

Establishing a culture in which students consolidate their learning and gain independence means helping teachers create classrooms where students take responsibility for their learning. Students who take that responsibility show it by working hard and using the information learned. You can observe cooperative learning, problem-based learning, and collaborative learning in elementary and secondary classrooms where student engagement is high. Students should be working hard and building knowledge. With teachers as catalysts for learning, the onus of the task falls on students, making them more self-reliant and better thinkers. So how do leaders enable this process? They educate teachers about these practices and encourage them to shift instruction to center on students with complex tasks.

Students cannot attend to teacher talk all day, retain what they hear, and apply it to new learning. Small-group discussions led by students increase comprehension and recall, making these discussions essential (Nystrand, 2006). The goal of consolidation is for students to apply the new knowledge and be able to think and work independently. Independent work is encouraged via the gradual release of responsibility, increased rigor and complexity, arts integration, field and guest experiences, and collaborative learning.

Gradual Release of Responsibility

When teachers gradually release responsibility, they seek to establish independent learning. This does not mean that students complete a worksheet independently. It means students take responsibility for their learning when they apply what the teacher has taught them and think and work independently. The gradual release of responsibility instructional framework purposefully shifts the cognitive load from teacher-as-model, to joint responsibility of teacher and learner, to independent practice and application by the learner (Pearson & Gallagher, 1983).

This increased student responsibility must be planned and practiced. During classroom visits for progress checks (with the goal of providing feedback that leads to teacher reflection and action), gradual release of responsibility occurs at any phase, even when students are engaged in independent learning activities. The observation form can help leaders observe this practice.

Just like teachers should encourage student-to-student interaction, leaders should encourage teacher peer review. Have teachers use the gradual release of responsibility observation form in figure 3.1.

Gradual Release of Responsibility Observation Form		
Record how long the teacher spends in each phase. Record evidence that indicates that instruction phase. Use the look-fors *as a guide.*		
Teacher: Date: Observer: Time in: Time out: Subject:		
	Teacher Moves	**Student Moves**
Phase one: *I do it.* (Direct instruction)	*Look-fors:* ☐ Ensures that the purpose explains the what, the why, and the how of the lesson ☐ Ensures the lesson is standards based ☐ Builds or activates background ☐ Models ☐ Uses think-alouds ☐ Keeps lesson brief	*Look-fors:* ☐ Knows what teachers expect him or her to know, understand, or do at the end of the lesson ☐ Asks questions ☐ Listens
Phase two: *We do it.* (Guided instruction)	*Look-fors:* ☐ Prompts, questions, facilitates, or leads through tasks ☐ Creates small groups based on specific needs ☐ Uses interactive instruction	*Look-fors:* ☐ Actively participates; asks and answers questions ☐ Works with teachers and students

Source: Claremont Academy, 2015.

Figure 3.1: Gradual release of responsibility observation form.   continued →

	Teacher Moves	Student Moves
Phase three: *You do it together.* (Collaborative learning)	*Look-fors:* ☐ Works with groups ☐ Clarifies misconceptions ☐ Provides feedback and support	*Look-fors:* ☐ Discusses, problem solves, negotiates, and thinks with peers ☐ Practices and applies learning ☐ Interacts with peers ☐ Uses language of standard and lesson ☐ Functions with individual accountability
Phase four: *You do it independently.* (Independent practice)	*Look-fors:* ☐ Provides feedback ☐ Checks for mastery and level of understanding ☐ Assesses	*Look-fors:* ☐ Draws on previous activities and learning ☐ Takes full responsibility for learning ☐ Works independently

*Visit **go.SolutionTree.com/leadership** for a free reproducible version of this figure.*

Leaders can use this form to see who is doing the most work in classrooms (teachers or students), judge who is taking the responsibility for high-quality work, initiate improvements, and help teachers clarify what they expect of students. Additionally, the observer can use what he or she sees in other classrooms to reflect on his or her own practice. Looking at instruction through a different lens creates a stronger practitioner.

Rigor and Complexity

Leaders know that to aid in consolidation, teachers must expose students to rigorous work. Systems thinking teachers inevitably run classrooms in which students study complex texts. They must use complex tasks to ensure that students listen and respond to questions and answers, and they must invite student inquiry and debate and encourage students to reference texts.

Rigor does not necessarily mean harder or more work but rather that the work makes students think. Good systems leaders use frequent progress checks and feedback to ensure that rigorous instruction and complex texts appear in every classroom. This feedback requires that teachers reflect on the kinds of instruction they provide, the types of responses they ask of students, and the complexity of their tasks.

During one meeting with kindergarten teachers at Claremont Academy to discuss their lesson plans, I noticed that most of their literacy unit focus was on foundational skills. When I asked where the literacy instruction was, one teacher stated that they needed to teach students the foundation before they could read. During a follow-up class visit during their read-aloud, I saw that students weren't directly interacting with the text.

Though independence is one of the goals in a systems thinking classroom, leaders may have to help teachers understand that they can't expect students to successfully read complex texts without guidance. With the assistant principal's help, a group of teachers at my school came up with a way to make sure that both teachers and students understand learning through complex texts. Figure 3.2 is the result of that reflection.

Text:		
Purpose of text:		
Learning target:		
	Questions or Purpose	**Annotations**
General understanding: Draw on the overall view, main ideas, or arguments		
Key details: The who, what, where, when, why, and how questions essential to understanding		
Vocabulary and text structure: Word choice to create mood or tone; focus on words and phrases; how author organized information; elements and structure		
Author's purpose: Genre, point of view, perspectives		
Inferential questions: Challenge to examine implicitly stated ideas or arguments		
Opinions, arguments, intertexual connections: Allows students to make claims or connections to other texts		

Source: Claremont Academy, 2015.

Figure 3.2: Guiding reading of complex text.

*Visit **go.SolutionTree.com/leadership** for a free reproducible version of this figure.*

Arts Integration and Field and Guest Experiences

Arts integration and field and guest experiences ensure another level of complexity toward the goal of learning consolidation. Leaders must promote the importance of learning relevance so students see how concepts work in everyday life. As principal at Claremont Academy, I made the expectation clear that every content teacher would take one trip or host one guest per quarter. There was a great outcry from teachers when I first implemented this enrichment policy. They already struggled with having so few hours in a day to teach. Fitting in trips seemed impossible, but they did it. The trips included activities like grocery shopping for budgeting, golfing for geometry, and geocaching for map reading. Remind teachers to explain to students the learning target—the purpose—and the relevance of each trip.

Leaders must vet these trips before teachers take them. Require teachers to include what experiences they will provide for their students and the outcomes they expect. Ask teachers to complete figure 3.3, which requires them to think through what students will learn, how that information applies to learning targets, and what its relevance and relatedness are to students.

Field experience	☐ Identify field experience (such as student trip or guest speaker) to consolidate learning.
	☐ Relate activity or assessment to learning expectation.
Activity and connection	Associated learning target:
	Relevance and relatedness to students:
	Learning evidence:
	Assessment:
Arts integration	☐ Identify arts integration to consolidate learning.
	☐ Relate activity or assessment to learning expectation.
Activity and connection	Associated learning target:
	Relevance and relatedness to students:
	Learning evidence:
	Assessment:

Source: Claremont Academy, 2015.

Figure 3.3: Field experience or arts integration rationale.

*Visit **go.SolutionTree.com/leadership** for a free reproducible version of this figure.*

Remind teachers that field experience and arts integration don't need to be labor intensive or expensive. For example, during a visit to my freshman daughter's American history class, I found the teacher projecting Walter Ellison's (1935) painting *Train Station*. The class conducted a close study of the painting. The teacher asked about its historical setting, the historical tone, the colors used, and how the painting supported texts that the students had read. The follow-up lesson was to read the poem "One-Way Ticket" by Langston Hughes (1949) and write about the connection among the social studies text, the painting, and the poem. All of this in a history class! Encourage teachers to use art as a primary source to help consolidate ideas. Integrating the arts and enabling students to integrate thinking across disciplines helps them apply and consolidate learning.

Collaborative Learning

Students working together consolidate their learning by applying previously learned concepts to new situations. Group work allows students to learn and interact with others while gaining a deeper understanding. During this work, all students are involved and teachers monitor student learning. The teacher can create ad hoc small groups for working toward deeper understanding or refinement. Students engage in independent practice after this additional time with peers.

Asking Driving Questions for Consolidating Learning

When students know how and when to use the information they have learned, they have consolidated their learning. Consolidation is a skill that teachers need to teach and that students must practice. Here are the five driving questions a systems thinking leader must consider when consolidating learning.

1. Have teachers moved to student-centered tasks that encourage students to assume the responsibility of high-quality work by persevering, initiating improvements, making revisions, and knowing what teachers expect of them?

2. Are teachers prepared for students to listen and respond to questions and answers, and do they invite student inquiry and debate while encouraging students to reference text?

3. Do teachers incorporate several opportunities for integration within and across disciplines?

4. Are students experiencing complex tasks to build understanding and mastery?

5. Do teachers provide opportunities for independent practice to demonstrate and verify understanding?

CHAPTER 4

LEADING LEARNING ASSESSMENT

If you don't know where you are headed, you'll probably end up someplace else.

—Douglas J. Eder

It was time to assess my school's assessment. I reflected on *Unstoppable Learning*'s formal leader driving questions, and I reflected on the required link between teaching and learning. Systems thinking leaders recognize that assessing is the foundational connection between teaching and learning (Fisher & Frey, 2015). I knew our school's system wasn't working due to the following.

- There was a disconnect between the standards and what teachers recorded in their gradebooks.

- Few teachers responded to an email about student opportunities to relearn and recover.

- According to the metric that measured students every five weeks, the percentage of students passing reading and mathematics was low.

- Gradebooks had too many zeros.

Leaders must help teachers see why learning assessment is important and determine what evidence of student learning should appear in gradebooks.

Systems thinking leaders ask themselves these driving questions for assessing learning:

- How are students informed of their progress throughout the unit?
- Were the results of the assessments consistent with the goals for the lesson or unit?
- What is the relationship between formative assessment and grades? Between summative assessments and grades?
- How do we inform families of their child's progress? What are the teacher's next steps? (Fisher & Frey, 2015, p. 176)

The principles of systems thinking—relationships, communication, responsiveness, and sustainability—are core parts of guiding assessment planning. Leaders will, with the principles, guide assessment and ensure its balanced creation. They also will give grading feedback while they lead learning assessment.

Guiding Assessment

It makes sense for leaders to address assessment while they help teachers plan official and operational curricula. In fact, it is the second stage of the Wiggins and McTighe (2005) backward design approach: decide what evidence to accept from students to assess their learning. It is important to create a balanced assessment blueprint during unit planning. If teachers develop a balanced assessment plan for measuring competency *before* instruction begins, then they can complete long- and short-term instructional plans toward the standard while continually assessing student understanding and individual student needs. The standards drive instruction and assessments are the maps leading there.

Leaders have a great deal of influence on this educational aspect, and many approaches are available. Douglas Reeves (2008) states, "If you want to make just one change that would reduce student failure rates, then the most effective place to start would be challenging prevailing grading practices" (p. 85). Teachers have to teach the standards, but leaders and teachers together decide what evidence is. Leaders can take Reeves's (2004) approach and get rid of the zero or try alternative assessment, which focuses on students' communication abilities (National Capitol Language Resource Center, n.d.) or go gradeless (Kohn, 2011). The good leadership practices of learning about students and their goals will come in particularly handy for this; leaders might consult them too about what evidence consists of. Questioning this aspect of learning can help teachers and students implement systems thinking. A new approach will require especially frequent check-ins, guidance, and feedback from leaders.

Teachers create assessments before the unit begins. This ensures that the teacher has planned backward from what he or she expects students to know and be able to do. The assessment plan includes a standards preassessment (to gauge for differentiation in instruction), all formative assessments, a midunit progress assessment, and the summative end-of-unit assessment. Excepting the schoolwide assessment, I give teachers full choice about what these assessments, and the texts that support the assessments, look like. Simply put, grading's true purpose is teachers knowing the following (Fisher & Frey, 2014).

- Where am I going? (Choosing expected standards)

- Where am I now? (Formative assessments)

- How do I close the gaps? (Differentiated approach)

Guiding Balanced Assessment Creation

In my school, teachers in all subjects create a balanced assessment plan for their units of study. A *balanced assessment* incorporates summative, formative, and interim assessment practices to improve standards-based learning. The difference among the three is crucial in creating the plan. While a formative assessment occurs almost daily and the summative occurs at the unit's end, the *interim assessment* is a formal protocol that captures data usually at the unit's midpoint.

Figure 4.1 is a self-reflection tool for teachers that helps ensure they can answer these questions.

Teacher: _____ Unit plan: _____ Date: _____	
Standards **Scope and sequence**	☐ I have ordered standards according to scope and sequence. ☐ I have identified learning targets.
Assessments	☐ I have created a preassessment. ☐ I have created formative assessments. ☐ I have created a summative assessment. ☐ Assessments align to standards. ☐ I have differentiated assessments.

Source: Claremont Academy, 2015.

Figure 4.1: Teacher self-reflection—balanced assessment evaluation.

*Visit **go.SolutionTree.com/leadership** for a free reproducible version of this figure.*

Giving Grading Feedback

Good leaders know that giving teachers feedback is a crucial part of systems thinking. Leaders help plan balanced assessments and then check teachers' progress throughout the year, just as teachers formatively assess students.

There must be an instructional shift when it comes to grading practices. Leaders must rethink and reform grading practices in order to assess student proficiency and standards mastery. They can help teachers overcome the traditional thoughts about grades (Guskey, 2011) as table 4.1 explains.

Table 4.1: Leading Away From Traditional Thoughts About Grades

Outdated Thought	New Thought That Leaders Can Convey to Teachers
Grades should provide the basis for differentiating students.	Ensure that teachers adhere to teaching standards, then articulate those standards and expectations to students (via classroom observations and feedback). There are fewer failures when teachers differentiate their instruction.
Grade distributions should resemble a normal bell-shaped curve.	This curve occurs when there are no interventions. Diversity is a crucial element in schools and therefore teachers are crucial interventions. Flatten the bell curve through purposeful differentiated instruction that attends to diversity.
Grades should be based on students' standing among classmates.	Remind teachers that an A grade tells nothing about a student's learning, nor does any grade present evidence of standards mastery. Encourage evidence-based assessment and discuss how teachers incorrectly weight the traditional grade scale (Reeves, 2004). It's important to be willing to let teachers try a different instructional approach, if necessary, and to communicate that willingness.
Poor grades prompt students to try harder.	No research proves this, and it unfortunately sets the precedent that grades are fixed. Encourage teachers to revisit content with a different strategy and allow students retakes and redos.

A collaborative team created our schoolwide grading system. The team created theories of action for grading policies and a gradebook-monitoring system. As the school's leader, I kept in mind and acted on the four systems thinking principles.

1. *Relationships* between teachers and principal made this change possible. The principal had to trust that teachers were capable of making a systems thinking change. The teachers had to trust that the principal would take their recommendations seriously and carry them out.

2. *Communication* about the initiative was crucial. Teachers used language in class, in the gradebook, and in conversations with parents that reflected what students had learned.

3. *Responsiveness* was fundamental to my position as leader. I needed to make sure I could field concerns and motivate teachers to continue the work.

4. *Sustainability* was imperative! The only way for this to continue was if teachers believed in the new grading vision. That came partly by way of different kinds of conversations that teachers were having with students and parents about achievement.

Leaders guide teachers regarding their approaches to grading, giving feedback, and communication during parent conferences.

Grading

Leaders can use a form to monitor adherence to a grading system like the one we implemented at Claremont Academy. I gave teachers feedback about the following.

- **How teachers label assessments:** It is important that assignments are labeled so that the viewer knows if it was classwork, homework, a unit test, or an interim assessment.

- **The frequency of monitoring a particular standard:** Teachers communicate midterm grades to students and parents, but even those shouldn't be a surprise to families. Intervention ideally occurs before this midpoint distribution, which requires teachers to take a high-level look at grades every week. Teachers frequently monitor student progress, just as school leaders frequently monitor classrooms.

- **Zeros and missing grades:** Systems thinking leaders know that student grades reflect student achievement. Therefore, teachers must consider how they will allow students to earn grades for missing assignments or assessments.

- **Additional retake opportunities:** Systems thinking classrooms focus on the big picture. In the case of grades, the goal is standards mastery. The gradebook system provides space for retakes. There are no minimum-grade requirements.

The running record in figure 4.2 (page 40) allows leaders to provide feedback on grading policies, students' mastery of standards, or individual student progress. A member of the leadership team reviews the gradebook, monitors the input, and provides comments in the "next steps" section.

Teacher: *Stan Derbased*

Grade and subject: *9—American Literature*

Color-coded by assignment	Assignment weight policy evident	Assignments listed by standards and description	Balanced assessment evident	Updated weekly	Standards addressed more than once	Minimal zeros / No blanks / Incomplete (INC) or missing (MSG) / Absence excused (EXC)	Retakes evident
Yes	*Yes*	*Standards only—no description*	*No*	*Yes*	*Yes*	*No*	*Yes*

Date: *November 30*

The expectation for students: *Standards mastery*

What is your plan for students who haven't successfully mastered a standard? The first assignment of Classroom 202 has 31 percent failing. Is differentiation necessary? Is there an opportunity for retakes? Classroom 206 had only a 5 percent failure rate. Have they mastered the standard? Overall, it seems that Classroom 202 is struggling more. What are you doing for them?

Classroom 206: Student JC only has one grade; the others are INC or EXC. What is the plan for him? Please start a multitiered system of support folder for him. He is unsuccessful due to his behaviors. Student AJ has no grades due to nonattendance. Have you spoken to the attendance counselor?

Standards are listed. You also need a brief explanation for reference and to indicate a variety of experiences and assignment types.

Color-coded by assignment	Assignment weight policy evident	Assignments listed by standards and description	Balanced assessment evident	Updated weekly	Standards addressed more than once	Minimal zeros No blanks Incomplete (INC) or missing (MSG) Absence excused (EXC)	Retakes evident
Yes	Yes	Yes	No— homework	Yes	Yes	Yes	Yes

Date: December 9

Next steps: Twenty percent of Classroom 202 did not master the summative assessment. What is the plan? Classroom 206 scored much better with most receiving As. Are the expectations different? Have you looked at the feedback that you are giving these students?

This shows no homework. Did you not assign it or not grade it?

Student AT has no grades. Is it attendance? What about student CB? These students need plans.

Source: Claremont Academy, 2015.

Figure 4.2: Leaders complete the teacher gradebook form.

This gradebook monitoring form also provides leaders a high-level view, which is essential for systems thinking. If teachers of the same subject and same grade level are working together on a unit, do their gradebooks look different? Why? To deepen instructional consistency and reinforce standards-based grading and learning, teachers of the same grade and subject must assess the same thing. Their gradebooks should mirror each other and, most important, mirror their instruction. This consistency and continual assessment of student progress allows the instructional leader to closely examine the effectiveness of the teacher's instruction and provide the feedback teachers need.

Giving Feedback

Pay attention to the work that teachers post in classrooms. What feedback, if any, do they write on it? I was surprised to see that most feedback was not actionable. It didn't provide guidance for students to act on, and it didn't move them toward standards mastery. I saw "A+," "Good work—keep it up!" and "85%." None of this informed the students of what they need to do differently or showed the teacher's intention to differentiate instruction. Help teachers give actionable feedback.

When properly given, feedback is one of the most powerful tools in instruction. Its purpose is to improve the quality of students' work toward standards mastery. Leaders hear verbal feedback during classroom visits and see written feedback on student work. When leaders hear or see feedback, they should ask themselves the following questions, then give their teachers actionable feedback.

- Is the feedback something students can take action on?
- Does the feedback move students toward the learning target?

After observations, give teachers the feedback form in figure 4.3 for their own reflection and ask them if what they provided led their students to better grasp the learning targets.

Teacher:	
Observer:	
Date:	
Feedback observations: *As you observe, take verbatim notes on the feedback the teacher gives to the students. Does this feedback encourage students to learn the objective, promote attempting or completing a task, or provide encouragement? Attach any artifacts, rubrics, and student work with feedback and the like.*	
Descriptive, Actionable Feedback	**Description of Task or Purpose**
• Feedback is actionable. • Oral and written feedback students receive is descriptive, timely, and based on shared criteria.	

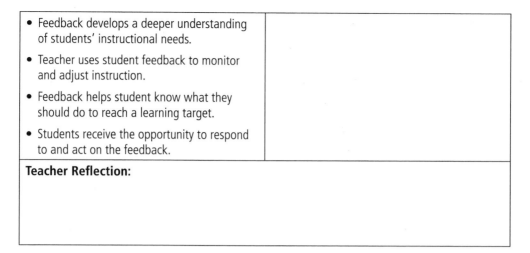

- Feedback develops a deeper understanding of students' instructional needs.
- Teacher uses student feedback to monitor and adjust instruction.
- Feedback helps student know what they should do to reach a learning target.
- Students receive the opportunity to respond to and act on the feedback.

Teacher Reflection:

Source: Adapted from Alaska Staff Development Network, n.d.

Figure 4.3: Teacher feedback—self-reflection.

Table 4.2 illustrates how teachers can replace traditional student feedback with actionable feedback.

Table 4.2: Replace Traditional Feedback With Actionable Feedback for Students

Traditional Feedback	Actionable Feedback
"A+"	"You've mastered this standard. Let's talk about enriching your understanding."
"Good work—keep it up!"	"Keep making those text-to-text connections."
"85 percent"	"Take another look at chapter 4; you struggled with some of those questions. Identify where you went wrong and reread the information you didn't understand. Provide the missing information."
"D"	"Following all the directions and explaining your thinking or showing your work will improve your grade."
"Sloppy work"	"It is easier for me to read your work when you put in more effort. Please review your work and identify errors, listing the page numbers where the information appears in the text."
"I've seen you do better."	"This standard has presented you with some challenges. Please plan to stay after school tomorrow so we can pinpoint where you need help. We will look at the rubric and analyze your work."

Leaders can offer another way to help teachers see clearly how actionable and standards targeted their feedback is. When returning an assignment to students with feedback, ask students to redo the same assignment using the feedback. Review the feedback and the assignment and complete the form in figure 4.4. Determine if the feedback is actionable and should produce a different result. Then look at the students' new work to determine if they progressed toward the goal. Systems thinking leaders ensure teachers are using actionable feedback. Teachers analyze student work and complete the form in figure 4.4 when submitting student work samples to school leaders.

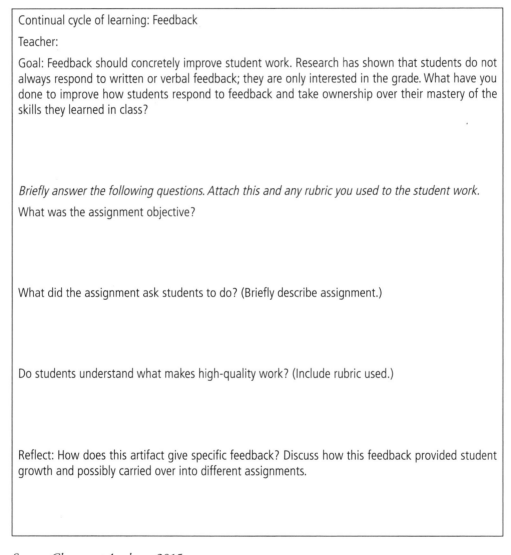

Continual cycle of learning: Feedback

Teacher:

Goal: Feedback should concretely improve student work. Research has shown that students do not always respond to written or verbal feedback; they are only interested in the grade. What have you done to improve how students respond to feedback and take ownership over their mastery of the skills they learned in class?

Briefly answer the following questions. Attach this and any rubric you used to the student work.

What was the assignment objective?

What did the assignment ask students to do? (Briefly describe assignment.)

Do students understand what makes high-quality work? (Include rubric used.)

Reflect: How does this artifact give specific feedback? Discuss how this feedback provided student growth and possibly carried over into different assignments.

Source: Claremont Academy, 2015.

Figure 4.4: Teacher feedback effectiveness form.

Communication During Parent Conferences

When meeting with a parent group, leaders should ask about children's progress. Parent responses may be similar: "His grades are okay," "She is a C student and does all of her homework," and "I don't get any bad reports from his teachers." Then ask what their children are *learning*. If leaders expect parents to become true partners in students' education, then they need to know what's really going on in the classroom, with the standards, and with what grades represent.

When leaders and their teachers discuss student achievement with parents, the language should center on the achievement standards. If a student received a D, advise the teacher to give parents specific feedback, just like he or she gave the student. Ensure that the teacher explains what the student's deficits are. Parents should get feedback that specifies what their children need to do to meet the standards.

Table 4.3 illustrates how teachers can replace traditional parent feedback with actionable feedback.

Table 4.3: Replace Traditional Feedback With Actionable Feedback for Parents

Traditional Feedback	Actionable Feedback
"He received a C on the fractions unit."	"He is able to add and subtract fractions with great accuracy, but has been struggling with ordering and comparing fractions."
"She is not completing her work."	"She had the chance, every Wednesday, to make up this work but did not take that opportunity. What can we do to get her here this Wednesday?"
"He wrote a really strong argumentation paper. He has a way with words."	"He wrote a really strong argumentation paper, using several reliable sources instead of any old site he found on the Internet."
"Good job!"	"She's done a great job solving the problem of the day. Please help her remember how important it is to explain, step-by-step, how she arrived at her answer."

When teachers return work to students, parents have no basis for comparison. Request that teachers, during parent conferences, show exemplars of at-level and above-level student work. Explain that they can share other students' work as long as they omit identifying information. A systems thinking leader always monitors what is expected. Accomplish this by asking teachers for parent conference samples and parent surveys, or by being visible during conference days and talking to parents.

Asking Driving Questions for Assessing Learning

Systems thinking leaders must drive behaviors until all stakeholders recognize that assessment is key to instruction. Systems thinkers know that without assessments, teachers have no map. The leader focuses on how teachers move their students after students receive data. How are students approaching their work differently as a result of feedback? Leaders must monitor and often revisit differentiation strategies. Consider these five driving questions about assessing learning.

1. Do all stakeholders realize that assessment is the key to the instructional and learning process because it connects thinking and learning?

2. How do leaders ensure that assessments are improving student mastery of standards and instruction?

3. Do teachers create plans to include diverse formative assessments that provide feedback about individual student levels of achievement and does the feedback inform future instruction?

4. Are all stakeholders aware of what high-quality instruction looks like? Do assessments and feedback lead students to desired outcomes?

5. Can students articulate what teachers expect of them, what the learning standards are, and make the changes necessary to lead to mastery?

CHAPTER 5

LEADING LEARNING ADAPTATION

*The price of doing the same old thing is
far higher than the price of change.*

—President Bill Clinton

At Claremont Academy, we established a climate and culture committee to improve our students' overall social emotional skills, creating a better climate and improving student achievement. During a meeting with the Climate and Culture Committee, one of the security officers announced, "The teachers are always late picking up their students from lunch."

Others began to chime in: "Yeah, that's right," and "I agree."

I looked at the teacher who leads the committee and said, "Okay, give me the data."

She said, "I believe the teachers are always on time because no one has called on the radio to report a late pick-up nor has anyone given me a piece of paper with the name of the late teacher, the date, and the time students were picked up."

What was my takeaway? Analyze the data and look for trends, just like Fisher and Frey (2015) recommend in *Unstoppable Learning*.

Systems thinking requires leaders to monitor classrooms so they can ensure that teachers and students have what they need to succeed. Sustainability, being a systems thinking principle, requires adaptation. Nothing is stagnant, least of all learning. Adjust plans, and encourage teachers to adjust plans, continually. Students will require accommodations—some will struggle and some will be gifted. When teachers adapt their instruction, more students will achieve.

Adaptation in schools takes the form of differentiation. It enables teachers to focus on the specific skills that various student groups need (Tyner, 2003). Small-group instruction, when teachers implement it effectively, requires students to work independently and teachers to have routines and practices in place. In chapter 4 (page 35), I talk about the kind of approaches that leaders should ensure teachers take: the gradual release of responsibility will help make the whole class more pliable.

Adaptations or accommodations for learning should happen for every student every day. While leading learning adaptation, ask these driving questions:

- How does the teacher leverage student errors to improve learning?
- What departures from the planned lesson did the teacher make, and why?
- Are there students who are being undersupported or oversupported?
- Are student supports and services aligned to promote academic growth?
- Are the supports and services the teacher provided consistent with the student's IEP goals?
- How does the school obtain feedback from families about successes and areas of needed improvement for supporting students? (Fisher & Frey, 2015, p. 177)

Leading those who are adapting learning is all about responsiveness, though obviously relationships, communication, and sustainability are important as well. The good leadership behavior of learning about students is foremost during this work. It is necessary when initiating differentiation planning, as well as when reading and implementing data to guide adaptations.

Initiating Differentiation Planning

Differentiation is a change in thinking in most schools. As Carol Ann Tomlinson (1999) points out, leaders can best support this change in practice by first developing a solid understanding of differentiated instruction, nurturing different teaching models, and encouraging teachers to apply differentiation with flexibility, creativity, and choice. Leaders will need quality professional development to understand differentiation and to learn about possible models. Teachers will also need quality professional development as well as time to collaborate, plan, and implement differentiation.

As a leader, ensure that teachers' lesson plans reflect student grouping based on some data. No single assessment tells teachers enough to make well-informed instructional decisions, so it is important to use multiple data sources.

When teachers plan and consider students' strengths and weaknesses, they place learners in groups that can best meet their needs. Let teachers know that they can form and dissolve groups as needs change (Opitz, 1998). Offer teachers the proactive tools in this chapter: student goal-setting forms, new lesson-plan documents, and a differentiation observation form. Using these tools, teachers can move from discovering what went wrong in the middle of the school year to planning weekly to meet their students' needs.

Reading and Implementing Data to Make Adaptations

A leader's intuition is a nice soft skill, but data-based trend analysis is key to high-performing schools. Good leaders check progress via different data tools and respond based on that information. Looking at trends is important because while they do not predict imminent outcomes, it is a starting point for strategic planning. Systems thinking requires leaders to consider what actions they should take as a result of the data. This is what adapting learning is all about.

School leaders can have coaching conversations during data meetings to improve teaching and learning. Ensure that teachers use quality data to adjust instruction and lesson plans. During these meetings, teachers focus on analyzing their progress monitoring tools, including formative assessments, global data, student data (such as standardized tests), and teacher peer observations. From there, leaders can encourage student ownership of their learning. It is a time to discuss the needs and abilities of specific students with the intention of identifying problems of practice and leveraging interventions.

Formative Assessments

Adapting learning around formative assessment is key because leaders must take action on the data. Sadler (1998) asserts that "Formative assessment refers to assessment that is specifically intended to provide feedback on performance to improve and accelerate learning" (p. 77). Researchers believe that the timeliness, flexibility, and ongoing nature of formative assessment techniques are most helpful not only in informing instruction for teachers but for closing achievement gaps for students and preparing them for the short- and long-term formative and summative benchmarks they need to attain (Hattie & Timperley, 2007; Sadler, 1989).

Global Data

Leaders are in a special position to look at and share schoolwide (known as *global*) data with all stakeholders. It is a starting place for adapting and communicating. The American Association of School Administrators (AASA, 2002) stresses that "districts play an important role in disseminating factual, timely information to parents about student achievement—the information parents care about most" (p. 32). Teachers and principals will need your coaching to become adept at communicating to the community about what data mean (AASA, 2002).

Student Data

Many states have moved to formative assessments by such organizations as Northwest Evaluation Association (NWEA), which measures student growth and attainment. Educators expect students to achieve a year's growth for every year they are in school. Every student has an NWEA growth target, and students who are behind are expected to catch up to meet attainment targets. Figure 5.1 shows midyear and end-of-year results.

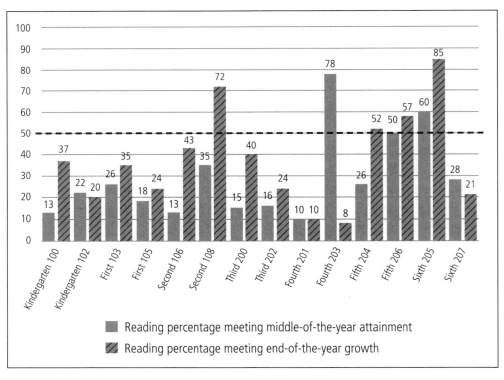

Source: Claremont Academy, 2015; NWEA, 2016. NWEA data were attained from and is representative of Claremont Academy and printed with permission from NWEA, 2016.

Figure 5.1: NWEA reading growth and attainment.

Leaders might ask themselves, and then their teachers, these three questions.

1. If the solid bars tell me the percentage of students meeting middle-of-the-year attainment, then most of the students are below grade level. The dotted line is the 50 percent mark. How can we adapt your teaching so that students catch up to grade-level standards?

2. If the striped bars tell me the percentage of students who have reached their end-of-the-year growth targets, then ten out of fourteen classes are below the halfway mark. How will we increase the rigor to ensure students achieve their growth targets?

3. It appears that some of the fourth-grade students are reaching their attainment targets, but they are not growing or learning. What are some possible hypotheses and reasons for this trend? How do we adapt for these high-achieving students?

Leaders ask teachers these questions to help them drill down and figure out how to meet students' needs. A conversation between a leader and a teacher about a student's needs might sound like this.

Leader: I can see that student AC has progressed well beyond her growth target and beyond the end-of-the-year attainment target. However, I'm concerned about what is going on with student AB.

Teacher: Student AB has been absent and struggling all year. She is very weak in mathematics.

Leader: Let's look at all data sources, student work, and attendance to decide next steps. What supports will you provide for students who did not meet their growth targets? What high-leverage teaching are you planning so students continue to grow and move? We can start with student AB.

When leaders meet with teachers about specific student data, they should take notes. Figure 5.2 (page 52) provides the notes from a conversation focusing on data sources and the planned adaptations.

Leaders should share these notes with the teacher and keep them in the teacher's file as well, so during frequent progress checks, they can recall what the plans were and ensure the teacher is enacting them.

Sources	Data: *Student has missed ten days of school.*
	• *Real and complex number systems: 28 percent*
	• *Algebraic thinking: 22 percent*
	• *Statistics and probability: 20 percent*
	• *Geometry: 30 percent*
	• *Missing assignments: Homework zeros in gradebook*
	Student work samples: Student is not using feedback from work given or feedback is ineffective.
	Contact log: Teacher has not made contact with home.
	No behaviors logged into system.
Adaptations	*Differentiation for all mathematics work with retakes until student achieves grade-level standards (five-week check-in)*
	Small-group or individualized tiered instruction in lesson plan (five weeks)
	Supplemental online mathematics program monitored weekly
	Parent and student check-in meeting weekly for homework and attendance (five weeks)
	Student goal setting completed with student that includes current scores, grades, barriers, and actionable steps to achieve greatness; weekly check-ins required

Source: Claremont Academy, 2015.

Figure 5.2: Notes from student-needs conversation between teacher and leader.

Teacher Peer Observation

Ask that teachers practice with the observation form in figure 5.3 and see how their peers are adapting to different student needs. A systems thinking leader encourages peer observation by supporting the process and meeting with teachers to reflect and look for trends. The leader supports the process by helping with scheduling or deciding which teachers should be observed. Sometimes administration must move the schedule to make observations possible. It is equally important for systems leaders to focus teachers on the kind of feedback they give during the observation process. Teachers needn't be nice or congenial; they must be honest so that colleagues grow in their practice. They should be collegial. Leaders can then focus on teacher reflections from two perspectives: what they learned from their observation and what they learned from what their peers observed.

Teacher:		
Observer:		
Date:		
Curriculum:	Evidence from student conversation:	
Teacher has identified learning targets clearly and students understand purpose of the task.		
Tasks:	Evidence from student work number one:	Evidence from student work number two:
Students are engaged and working on a task that is appropriately challenging.		
Grouping:	Evidence of groups:	
Students are working in small groups.		
Assessment:	Evidence (for example, questions, exit slips, or presentation):	
Teacher has a strategy to gather information about student achievement.		
Teacher group:	Evidence of student conversation:	
Teacher interacts with students during lesson.		
Reflections: What feedback can I share with my colleague?	Reflections: What can I take back to my classroom?	

Source: Claremont Academy, 2015.

Figure 5.3: Teacher adaptation or differentiation form.

*Visit **go.SolutionTree.com/leadership** for a free reproducible version of this figure.*

The teacher adaptation or differentiation form offers a way to achieve open dialogue about adapting learning practices. It creates an internal learning community. Cristi Alberino, a researcher at the University of Pennsylvania's Graduate School of Education, believes teachers should "use one another for professional development" (Education World, n.d.). A systems thinking approach encourages teachers to examine each other's practices and reflect on their own. A leader understands the benefits of peer observations and maintains the focus on student learning. When observers examine this document carefully, it directs them to talk to students and look at student work. Because the visits are not evaluative, teachers have an opportunity to observe classroom practices through a different lens than they may be used to. As long as there is an established positive relationship, this practice creates shared responsibility and an increase in student achievement.

Student Ownership

When I was a middle school student, we received our standardized-test scores on the last day before break. We never had an opportunity to discuss scores with our teachers. We never knew exactly what they meant. As students, we just wanted to be above grade level. We had no idea about strengths or weaknesses unless they were mathematical concepts. So, we had very little direction. All we really knew was that the Iowa Test of Basic Skills would become part of our permanent record. School would start again in September and we would already be assigned a reading group. We knew the scores were used for tracking. Leaders can advise teachers to avoid this same experience for their students.

One way is to have students set goals for themselves. It helps them take responsibility for their own learning and moves them toward the independence that is so valuable in a systems thinking classroom. In any way they can, leaders should encourage students to match their academics and behaviors with the student they want to be.

Figure 5.4 is one form leaders can provide to teachers for their students. To move themselves toward the good leadership goal of learning about teachers and students, leaders should take a look at these completed forms.

Make sure teachers are free to develop their own student goal forms, but require a few key points.

- Share all data and have students set goals (attendance, suspensions, standards mastery, test scores, grades, GPA). Ensure that students create realistic goals. If a student has poor attendance, a class grade of 96 percent in five weeks is highly unlikely.

- Begin every goal sentence with an actionable word. ("*Complete* homework every night.")

- Create strategies that lead to success by discussing barriers during plan development. ("Write down all assignments and do my homework when I first get home.")

- Include a timeline with weekly check-ins. Be willing to adapt if needed. ("How am I doing?")

- Make it a family plan. During the parent conference, ask if students have shared their goals. Have parents share how they encourage their children to meet their goals.

My Goals This Week

Name: _____   Date: _____

I. Beginning of year

	Standard		My Scores	Goal	Ten Weeks
Attendance					
Reading					
Mathematics					
Science					
Suspension					
Grades	A–Reading	A–Mathematics			

II. What will you do to reach your goals?

Complete all of my homework every night.

Go to bed at 10:30 p.m. every night.

III. What do you need to do to reach your goals?

Write down all my homework before I leave school.

Text a friend if I forget something.

Stop playing video games on my phone and go to bed when my mother tells me.

IV. Check-in

Teacher will X each box when homework is completed for that day.

Monday	Tuesday	Wednesday	Thursday	Friday

Parent signature: *Tamu Smith*

V. Family agreement: What can I do to help my child meet his or her goals?

Weekly check-ins with my child

VI. What are possible barriers?

My other familial obligations

Source: Claremont Academy, 2015.

Figure 5.4: Sample student goal form.

Asking Driving Questions for Adapting Learning

Systems thinking leaders adapt their practice based on data. Adapting is really drilling down and figuring out how to meet students' needs. Systems thinking leaders always think about how they can influence organizations and the people within them to improve learning. The five driving questions a systems thinking leader must consider about adapting follow.

1. Do I, as the leader, understand the rationale for adaptive learning?

2. How will I assist teachers analyze data that they can transfer into action?

3. How will I provide time for teachers to transition from professional development to safe practice?

4. How will I nurture and support the cadre of teachers who are early adopters?

5. How will I monitor classrooms to ensure groups are flexible and data are current?

CHAPTER 6

LEADING LEARNING MANAGEMENT

Human behavior flows from three main sources: desire, emotion, and knowledge.

—Plato

I was in the hall speaking with a student when I heard the sounds of a serious commotion coming from a classroom. The students became silent when I opened the classroom door. I gave the students my "principal look," and the teacher said, "We are having a hard time settling down this morning."

Research shows that a teacher's actions in the class have twice the impact on student achievement as do school policies regarding curriculum, assessment, staff collegiality, and community involvement (Marzano & Marzano, 2003). This first-year teacher wanted to embrace the faculty pledge (of taking responsibility for providing every student skills that turn them into lifelong learners and creating a school culture geared toward integrity and excellence), but something wasn't going well.

The teacher came to my office during his break and explained that he had succeeded at everything in his life thus far: attending an Ivy League college, earning perfect mathematics SAT scores, and competing well in athletics. He didn't understand why he struggled with classroom management. If only teaching were so easy. Luckily, the teacher was looking at himself instead of at his students.

Students and teachers look to their principal to lead them to learning. That includes not only curricula and assessment but a less concrete and very important part of education—social and emotional learning. Maintaining a culture of learning rests on the leader's shoulders. Visit classrooms, give teachers feedback, and address learning gaps. Collaborate with staff to create a schoolwide climate vision statement. Require classroom management plans from all teachers so they can help students develop self-awareness and manage their own behavior. Support teachers in conflict resolution management. Finally, implement restorative practices; these are essential in a school. Leaders should do all of this in tandem with students' families.

Unstoppable Learning (Fisher & Frey, 2015) recommends that leaders manage leading by asking these driving questions:

- How does the management of the classroom facilitate student learning?
- Do students know the ways of work in the classroom?
- Does the teacher contribute data to resolve problematic student behaviors? (p. 178)

Leading and managing are not very different. Leading learning management houses these principles: relationships, communication, responsiveness, and sustainability. All efforts toward this end must be sustainable and they're all about building positive relationships. Leading these management efforts asks leaders to provide explicit task introduction, guidance and feedback, and frequent progress checks. Leaders can focus on learning who students are as a way to round out efforts to establish systems that encourage social and emotional learning and academic learning.

Establishing Systems That Encourage Social and Emotional Learning

According to the Collaborative for Academic, Social, and Emotional Learning (CASEL, n.d.):

> Social and emotional learning (SEL) is the process through which children and adults acquire and effectively apply the knowledge, attitudes, and skills necessary to understand and manage emotions, set and achieve positive goals, feel and show empathy for others, establish and maintain positive relationships, and make responsible decisions.

Principals must lead everyone in the school family—faculty, staff, students, and families—toward SEL.

Schoolwide Climate and Expectations Establishment

Systems thinking leaders establish a shared agreement with all staff members, much like teachers do with students in the class. It is the vision for the behaviors they expect from the faculty. The climate in a school must center on respect, with everyone feeling responsible for their actions. Leaders must recognize that a positive school climate is important. When they work with staff to develop expectations, all stake-holders expect staff to do the right thing.

Systems thinking leaders understand the importance of building relationships with teachers and inspiring them to create a collective agreement for the school building. It is vital that this vision articulate some core values, such as, "We as a school agree on purpose, respect, and integrity." By taking time to develop shared understandings, you have a starting point for student and teacher behaviors. See the suggested behaviors listed in figure 6.1.

Shared Understanding: We understand that in order to motivate and hold our students accountable for success, we must motivate each other and hold ourselves accountable for success.

Expectations

Know Your Purpose

Understand that all students are capable of behaving appropriately.

Enforce your classroom management plan consistently and fairly.

Accept responsibility to take all steps to ensure students learn to do so.

Take steps to build trusting relationships with and among all students by facilitating circles; have restorative conversations with students after incidents.

Take steps to build trusting relationships with families.

Show Respect

Understand that we lead our students and each other by example.

Monitor student behavior and provide consistent positive feedback (4:1 ratio of positive to negative or corrective) to students who choose to comply with expectations.

Monitor student behavior and quickly provide clear direction, narration, and corrective action in accordance with school policy in a calm, respectful manner when students choose not to comply.

Be mindful of tone and delivery when we speak to one another.

Show Integrity

Remember the Golden Rule.

Attend to meetings or pick-ups on time instead of waiting to start meetings or pick-ups at the specified time.

Engage in activities, projects, dialogues, and so on. Recognize that your voice counts.

Adhere to requests in a timely manner and communicate challenges with deadlines prior to the deadlines.

Figure 6.1: Staff and leaders collaborate to create expectations.

From guiding teachers in expectation setting that addresses their own behavior, it isn't a big leap to the next expectation leaders should make clear: classroom management.

Classroom Management Plans

Leithwood, Louis, Anderson, and Wahlstrom's (2004) review of multiple studies finds that leadership accounts for one-fourth of all school-related variation in student learning, second only to the quality of curriculum and instruction. Leaders can guide teachers toward successful classroom management in a few ways. One is to clarify who manages specific types of behaviors. Systems thinking leaders work with teachers to delineate what behaviors are handled in the classroom; teachers are students' first point of contact. Good behavior should be praised and poor behavior should be acknowledged and corrected immediately. Teachers can acceptably address some in the classroom but some require office intervention. A typical approach might align with table 6.1.

Table 6.1: Specify Who Manages Student Behaviors

Classroom-Managed Behaviors	Office-Managed Behaviors
Failing to comply	Possessing weapons or look-alike weapons
Coming unprepared	Injuring (or threatening to injure) students or staff
Missing homework	Displaying gang-related behaviors
Not wearing uniform	Fighting (not horseplay)
Arguing	Stealing
Talking or making excessive noise	Recording inappropriate behaviors
Engaging in horseplay	Exhibiting sexual behaviors
Being tardy	Bullying
Misusing phone or other technology	Cursing at staff
Displaying off-task or disruptive behaviors	Leaving school without permission
Picking on peers	Possessing or using alcohol or drugs
Cursing or name-calling	Repeating classroom-managed behaviors
Leaving classroom without permission	Displaying other seriously disruptive or dangerous behaviors
Committing academic dishonesty or cheating	
Displaying other inappropriate behaviors	

Source: Claremont Academy, 2015.

Leaders make it clear to teachers that many students arrive at school without a sense of what it means to be a contributing member of a group. Teachers must often convey this to students by building lessons where students role play and choose appropriate behaviors in given situations. Those who do not naturally teach this will struggle with this idea of teaching SEL.

Providing training that focuses on explicit instructions that teachers can use in classroom management is vital to sustaining schoolwide management. Kevin

Haggerty of the Social Development Research Group says the best teaching builds a protective environment. Experts say "That protective environment can prevent [the self-destructive behaviors] that lead to delinquency, drug use, and dropping out" (Elias, Bruene-Butler, Blum, & Schuyler, 1997).

When teachers have received sufficient training and created collaborative faculty expectations, and the leader has communicated to teachers the distinction between classroom-managed and office-managed behaviors, the leader should ask teachers to create a classroom plan and meet with them about it. Offer help if they need it. The plan requires that teachers think through all their routines, incentives, and consequences. Creating this plan requires teachers to figure out how they can provide students with leadership opportunities. Systems thinking leaders realize that when teachers establish stability in a classroom, they can clearly identify and analyze behavior trends and pinpoint students who may need additional supports. Figure 6.2 is a sample classroom management plan. The plan incorporates a schoolwide strategy as well. It is crucial that the school leader communicates a shared approach to set the tone for the plan.

Classroom Management Plan

Teacher: *Javier Plan*

Date: *October 1*

Subject or grade: *Grade 5*

Subject or grade: *Grade 5*

My philosophy: Your beliefs about classroom management. Include a description of your teaching beliefs.

My philosophy is that everyone, the teacher and the students, should treat each other and speak to each other with respect. Students will learn how to celebrate their successes and the success of others. In addition, they will learn to accept when they do not excel and how to think about doing better.

Students, with modeling and practice, will learn to identify conflicts that they can ignore and those that they need to address. Students will learn how and where to resolve conflicts, understanding that the teacher can help them if they are at an impasse. They should understand that the teacher will be the final authority on unresolved issues.

Finally, students will learn to embrace our class motto, "Hand in Hand, Together We Can," in order to understand that success is a group effort.

Room arrangement: How is your class organized? It is important to think about room organization when setting up a class.

Completed on a separate sheet of paper.

Figure 6.2: Sample classroom management plan.   continued →

Classroom signals: How do you communicate nonverbally with students?

- *Teacher holds hand in air for quiet.*
- *Teacher claps patterns to get attention.*
- *Teacher uses some American Sign Language signs for <u>sorry</u>, <u>thank you</u>, <u>teacher</u>, <u>student</u>, and <u>bathroom</u>.*
- *Teacher counts on fingers associated with a particular action for quiet preparation for leaving the classroom.*
- *Teacher rings a bell for students to transition to centers.*

Classroom rules: Include a max of five.

- *Treat others the way you want to be treated.*
- *Listen when others are talking.*
- *Follow directions.*
- *Keep hands and feet to yourself.*
- *Smile often!*

Consequences: Explain what happens if someone breaks a classroom rule.

Apologize to person or class for infraction.

Repeat infractions (more than two): Move down a color. (green = go ☺; yellow = I can do better ☺; orange = I am asking for attention the wrong way 💔; red = I need a reminder from home ☹)

Orange color: No recess. Explain the problem to the teacher.

Red color: No recess. Explain the problem to the teacher and parents.

Rewards or incentives: What are your classroom incentives?

Individual	Group	Whole Class
Attendance: Every day, on time. At the end of the month students receive a special prize. *Behavior: Hold a Fun Friday with educational games.* *Schoolwide SEL strategy: Have special recognition and special privileges.*	*Behavior: Fun Friday*	*Attendance: If the entire class comes every day on time for the month, we will have a class celebration for parents and students.* *Behavior: Fun Friday*

Entry routines: What do students do upon arrival to your room? Include morning routines.

- *In an orderly line, receive the breakfast from the cafeteria worker, say thank you, line up, and wait for the rest of the class outside our classroom door.*
- *Get a place mat from the yellow table to place your breakfast on your desk.*
- *Place milk in the middle of the table and put coat and backpack on the back of your chair.*
- *During breakfast, listen to or watch the story or lesson. Be prepared to answer questions about the details.*
- *After breakfast, wait for your table to be called to throw away your trash and put your things in your locker.*
- *Carry your milk to the trash first. Come back and gather the rest of your trash.*

End-of-day or -period routine: What do students do during the last five minutes of class or the day?

- *Select the student of the day for the next day. (Just pull a stick out of the box.)*
- *Students are called by tables to get backpacks and homework journals from personal tubs.*
- *Line up in order.*

Homework policy _____

- *Homework is due the next day or, for extended projects, the assigned date.*
- *Parents must sign homework to indicate that they have seen and checked it.*

Missing assignment policy _____

Student will receive one opportunity to make up an assignment.

Student absence and work policy _____

The teacher will keep a folder with the student's homework assignment in the classroom until his or her return on the next day. The work will be due the day following the return.

If the student is absent two or more days, the teacher will contact the parent and make arrangements for the parent to pick up the homework.

continued →

Procedures: What do students do when they . . .? Can students talk during . . . ? What does student work behavior look like?

Transitioning: *Teacher claps a rhythm. Students stop what they are doing, repeat the rhythm, and then listen for instruction. Teacher will ring a bell for center transition. Students are required to track with their eyes the person who is talking.*

Lining up: *Students will be given a line order based on height. There will be a line leader and a door holder who will be second in line. Students will take turns.*

Turning in work: *Table captains will collect classwork. Each student will place his or her homework in the homework basket at the beginning of the day.*

Finishing a task: *Students may read solo from the leveled reader boxes, or select something from their "I'm done" folders. When they have to use the washroom, they raise a fist and pretend to knock on a door (silent signal for washroom request).*

Passing in the hall: *Students keep their arms by their sides. They form two straight lines and look at the back of the head of the person in front of them.*

Sharpening pencils: *Teacher sharpens all pencils before or after school and during prep.*

Asking for help: *Students raise their hands. No shouting for the teacher. If it is not a quiz or a test, they may feel free to ask someone at their table.*

Answering a question: *Students answer in full sentences and speak so the whole class can hear and learn from them.*

Getting materials: *The table captains and the student of the day will share distribution duties. When students need something to complete an assignment, they will ask the table captain. If the captain cannot get the required item, the captain should raise his or her hand and ask the teacher for it.*

Class climate: How does your classroom feel? Is it safe for students?

- *Teacher will model how to talk with someone with whom they disagree and then show them the part of the room that is designated for "talking it out."*
- *Students will practice getting to know each other by finding and talking with people sharing the same birth month and playing get-to-know-you games, circle time after recess, and role playing for restorative practices.*

Parent communication _____

The teacher employs monthly newsletter, emails to parents with that capability, phone calls, and parent workshops.

Positive Climate Monitoring

Leaders can apply systems thinking to social and emotional learning as well as to academic learning. Ask teachers to log positive student behavior. During afternoon announcements, leaders can recognize some students for good behavior. Encourage teachers to use positive narration for students exhibiting positive behaviors: "Shawn is quiet in line and ready to go." Check progress frequently and notice the trends. When I have seen the big picture, it inspires my students to strive for excellence in the areas where teachers recorded a spike in negative behavior.

In line with the gradual release of responsibility, encourage teachers to do the same with behavior. Teachers can empower students by having them monitor their own behavior, recording a tally mark every time they engage in an off-task behavior. This can be a tough transition. Instead of frequently saying, "Let's focus," or "Okay, people," there may be a spike in off-task behavior. Once teachers reflect on the totals with students, they will hopefully see a decrease in the behaviors. Ask teachers to keep this in mind: "If the goal is to have children take responsibility for their behaviors, teachers must allow students to *make decisions about what is right and wrong*" (Hardin, 2008, p. 143).

Conflict Resolution and Restorative Practices

Just as some teachers will struggle with SEL efforts, not every student will respond positively. Regardless, all infractions should include restorative practice, which "are processes that proactively build healthy relationships and a sense of community to prevent and address conflict and wrongdoing" (Advancement Project, American Federation of Teachers, National Education Association, & National Opportunity to Learn Campaign, 2014, p. 2). Students learn conflict-resolution skills when leaders implement practices such as conferences and peer mediation (Blood & Thorsborne, 2005).

When a school embraces restorative practices, all adults—principal, clerk, custodians, coaches, cafeteria staff, librarian, teachers, parents, volunteers—learn to bring a holistic approach to a school. Well-trained staff see the impact of students looking at the effects of their behavior. Systems thinking leaders and their staff understand that these practices attempt to repair the harm done.

If all students want to be successful, then why are some successful and others unsuccessful? Often, it's disconnection. Students who feel disconnected from their school are more likely to behave dangerously or engage in other risky actions during school (Blum, McNeely, & Nonnemaker, 2002). Again, the importance of communication, relationship building, and responsiveness, which support systems thinking classrooms, becomes clear, as does the importance of encouraging teachers to help students see the relatedness and relevance of what they're learning. Provide teachers with a plan to help them successfully use restorative practices in their classrooms. Academic learning coexists with social and emotional learning. Leaders should make sure the following systems are in place.

Establishing Systems That Ensure Academic Learning

"What's not inspected can't be expected" was a famous line Joyce Bristow would quote to the thirty-five principals under her leadership as the instructional officer for Chicago Public Schools Area 16. She would often stress the importance of monitoring throughout the school year, saying, "It is not good enough to have a great plan and hope for the best; the bigger job is how you are going to monitor all the things you put in place" (J. Bristow, personal communication, August 2002). A systems thinking leader is not only a part of the planning process; he or she must also monitor expected outcomes and compare them with actual outcomes. Monitoring for consistency between goals and actions is every leader's responsibility; that way, everyone can strive to align his or her efforts for a greater chance at success. Leaders must also plan to step in to address gaps, should that be necessary.

When school leaders have designed planning and monitoring systems, teachers know what their leaders expect of them and why it is important. Teachers should not have to guess how they should go about achieving schoolwide goals. Leaders can see successful planning's outcomes by several means: assessments, formal visits, and informal visits. Systems thinking leaders follow up with feedback and plans to address gaps.

Assessment

During my tenure as a principal in Chicago, my school's goal was to have at least 70 percent of students attain mathematics learning goals. I requested pretests and benchmark assessments. Teachers adjusted their lessons as a result of the assessment data they obtained. They would continue concentrating on the standards, but instead of teaching what they *thought* students needed, they could teach what the students *actually* needed. About four weeks into the term, I checked progress.

Informal and Formal Visits

I always look for confirmation of student learning when I walk around the school. A leader has his or her finger on the pulse of the school. To really know what is going on, a leader must be present in the classrooms—either through informal classroom visits, formal observations, instructional rounds, or learning walks. One of the best ways to truly understand the goings-on of the school is to be present in the classrooms in a nonevaluative way.

As an administrator in a large district, I was too often pulled away from teachers and instructional leaders due to meetings, mandates, paperwork, budget issues, and many other things. I realized that I was getting bogged down in operations management and wasn't present in the true mission of the school—the teaching and learning. I had to get out of my office and into the classrooms.

Our collaborative teams conducted learning walks to monitor the implementation of our schoolwide practice, visiting classrooms to collect observational data—for example, whether the practice was evident, whether we saw student work that reflected the practice, and whether instruction was improving—and to give feedback to the practicing teacher.

Being present in the classroom is also the best way to connect with the students. A one-minute interaction with a student says, "You are important to me. Your academic success is a priority." This communication helps create a positive learning culture. Leaders can encourage the school's leadership team to adopt a class. I adopted a fourth-grade class and agreed to check in almost daily. With the teacher, I monitored attendance, behavior, and grades. I got to know these students well. They were excited to tell me what they were learning and that they had been at school every day. Over the year, attendance rates improved, fewer students received failing grades, and parents visited the school more frequently. My conversations with the students centered on them becoming successful students and great thinkers. The change was impressive. As an instructional leader, these conversations allowed me to gauge if the students knew the purpose of their learning and how they could improve their learning to meet their goals. The district office will have many needs, but the reports and emails should wait until you've visited classrooms and have a pulse on your school's instructional program.

When a leader is adept at conducting informal learning visits, he or she can connect informal observations to the state-mandated standards to determine whether students are meeting those standards. Think through what the standards expect—what students should be able to do on grade level by the end of the year—and if these outcomes are easily observable. If the standard is RL.2.1, "Ask and answer such questions as who, what, where, when, why and how to demonstrate understanding of key details in a text," (NGA & CCSSO, 2010) then a systems thinking leader is looking for evidence of students using the text to answer questions. Using the 3-2-1, or PQS, chart, a leader could write statements that support this standard. This is an example:

- P: I like the way students at the first table were finding words in the text to describe the main character.

- Q: I wonder if the students in group three could identify the main character; could they find words to describe him in the text?

- S: Consider pairing students strategically as opposed to homogeneously.

Leaders know what to look for when observing teaching and learning. Chapter 3 (page 27) explains those look-fors.

Feedback

Follow up classroom visits by consistently giving teachers feedback. This reflects two of the systems thinking principles: communication and responsiveness. Consistent feedback supports teaching and learning improvement. Research has found that when providing feedback, "it is important to focus on the daily teaching practice, more specifically, the subject content, the subject pedagogical content knowledge and the students' learning processes of a specific subject" (van Veen, Zwart, & Meirink, 2012, p. 17). The authors also note that "when teachers develop with respect to these aspects of content, an increase in teacher quality and student learning results" (van Veen et al., 2012, p. 12).

It is important to note that routines and procedures are in place for this feedback; purposeful planning addresses that need. One teacher may have excellent management practices; another teacher may be the school's resident collaborative grouping expert. Recognize these teachers and encourage them to share their talents with other staff members. Procedures such as peer observations allow for great communication. As with students, feedback allows teachers to practice, get better, and master the new learning. Again, feedback must be actionable; leaders cannot monitor the implementation of new learning and provide feedback if they are not aware of what it should look like in practice. Implementing instructional feedback using a 3-2-1, or PQS, chart as part of the informal learning walk helps strengthen a teacher's instructional practices. A completed 3-2-1 chart could look something like figure 6.3. Leaders should provide feedback this way whenever they can. They are thus able to identify quick wins by looking at strengths and immediately offering suggestions.

Praise can help teachers see the value in planning, and it encourages them to continue this behavior in the future. Richard M. Ryan and Edward L. Deci's (2000) research proves that positive reinforcement helps reaffirm the future pursuit of goals. Using the 3-2-1 model, leaders quickly, explicitly connect learning to planning for teachers. The praise ideally relates to an action or outcome that required the teacher to plan ahead; the questions set teachers to thinking about other ways they can succeed in class with preparation; and the suggestion requires forethought to implement.

Frequent progress checks, such as those done with the 3-2-1 chart, are the responsibility of every principal. They can consist of walking around talking to students and visiting classrooms, or they may involve designing sophisticated information systems to check on performance. Successful leadership—and successful teachers and students—stems from purposeful planning and steering.

Teacher: *Ms. Lovetoteach*
Date: *October 30*
Observer: *Mrs. Lovetolead*
3 Praises
You have clearly identified the learning standards and written them on the board.
I noticed five students were working on the computer on the same standard.
I see that everyone else was reading a piece of text silently.
2 Questions
How do you ensure your students can explain the standard and why it is important?
Have students preread the text or heard it read smoothly?
1 Suggestion
Consider allowing students to partner read to build fluency.

Figure 6.3: Implement instructional feedback using a 3-2-1 (PQS) chart.

*Visit **go.SolutionTree.com/leadership** for a free reproducible version of this figure.*

Gaps

Of course, responsiveness is key when leading learning. When leaders find a gap between teacher efforts and school-improvement goals, they must take action immediately. Planning ahead enables that: "When teachers in a school perceive that they receive more support from their principal, they are more willing to learn and try new ideas, and to participate in collective professional activities in a more active manner" (Bryk & Schneider, 2002). One-on-one teacher meetings is one approach I took when I saw gaps in mathematics benchmark data. I created the driving questions form in figure 6.4 (page 70) to give these meetings direction.

When I saw a learning gap and had these individual conversations with teachers, they changed the way they designed their instruction, and this in turn changed the way the students responded to learning. Teachers placed students in fluid groups and could identify what they were learning. I could clearly see mastery of standards reflected in teachers' gradebooks, and it started with my plans to make sure I knew what was going on in the classrooms. Creating learning systems means the leader is not only setting high expectations but also monitoring learning and participating in conversations to sustain continuous improvement.

How do you know when students are learning? _____

_____

Are all students learning? Who is showing the greatest growth? The least? _____

_____

How does that knowledge impact your planning and teaching? _____

_____

What are the next steps for students who have mastered the standard or objective? What are the next steps for students who have not mastered the standard or objective? _____

_____

Figure 6.4: Driving questions to ask during one-on-one teacher meetings.

*Visit **go.SolutionTree.com/leadership** for a free reproducible version of this figure.*

Good leaders anticipate errors and know that gaps are likely to appear in the teaching of first-year and new-to-the-district teachers. Some veterans become complacent. They may no longer put effort into planning new instruction for their students but instead use instinct and outdated approaches. All lesson plans should reflect the needs of the classroom's current students. Again, plan on being familiar with students, teachers, and classroom instruction in order to address any gaps.

Asking Driving Questions for Managing Learning

Support from a systems thinking leader is critical to ensuring that everyone consistently implements improvement efforts schoolwide and sustains them in the long run. Students flourish in well-managed classrooms. Improved management skills and positive mindsets lead to higher SEL levels and greater achievement. As leaders observe changes, they will reflect on which strategies are effective, make improvements, and celebrate all accomplishments. A systems thinking leader must consider these five driving questions about managing learning.

1. Have I developed a shared vision in which all staff members understand school climate development is critical for school improvement?

2. Am I providing the support that teachers and staff need to implement new practices?

3. How will I review teachers' individual classroom management plans and implementation strategies? How will I ensure teachers carry out the selected strategies as intended?

4. How will I analyze data to identify strong climate areas, as well as areas that need improvement?

5. How will I move the school to a safe, supportive environment that uses conflict resolution and restorative practices?

A Final Word on Systems Thinking and Leading Learning

This book's fundamental message centers on the idea that a leader recognizes the imperative of creating channels for growth and opportunity to lead learning. A true leader understands how all these elements connect. Look at data trends and make decisions because the real core of systems thinking and leading is the relentless pursuit of greatness; provide the best situations to link the systems together.

I remember reading *A Seed Is a Promise* by Claire Merrill (1990). What I remember most about this book was that the seed went on quite an adventure when the wind blew it from its flower. It was nourished despite bumps, and it became a beautiful flower. Teachers took up their profession because they are passionate about teaching. If leaders nourish them properly, they bloom into great teachers. Leaders know the job of educating students is quite an arduous task. Systems thinking leaders are up to this task. Figure E.1 can help leaders reflect on their own strengths and weaknesses as systems thinking leaders.

What went well during school prep that I did on my own?

_____

What went well during school prep that I worked on with teachers?

_____

What will I do differently next time?

_____

Figure E.1: Principal or school leader self-reflection.   continued →

Did teachers appear prepared and aware of my expectations?

_____

What evidence proves that?

_____

If not (or if not all did), what can I do to help make that happen?

_____

Did students master the standards?

_____

What evidence proves that?

_____

Did I follow through on my faculty, staff, student, parent, and community communication plans?

_____

Did these parties follow up on my communication efforts? If not, how can I help make that the case?

_____

Did I provide specific, timely feedback to teachers and other staff?

_____

Did I check progress throughout the unit or year? What evidence proves that?

_____

What did I find and how was it useful?

_____

What errors was I able to anticipate?

_____

What can I take to my superintendent?

_____

What can I take to my teacher teams?

_____

*Visit **go.SolutionTree.com/leadership** for a free reproducible version of this figure.*

A systems thinker understands the connected aspects of leading. A systems thinking leader knows the serious thought that goes into improving teaching and learning. In the words of John D. Rockefeller, "Don't be afraid to give up the good to go for the great" (Biography.com editors, 2016).

References and Resources

Adams, G., Lenz, B. K., Laraux, M., Graner, P., & Pouliot, N. (2002). *The effects of ongoing communication between teachers and adolescents with disabilities* (Research Report No. 12). Lawrence: University of Kansas, Institute for Academic Access. Accessed at http://files.eric.ed.gov/fulltext /ED469545.pdf on August 11, 2016.

Advancement Project, American Federation of Teachers, National Education Association, & National Opportunity to Learn Campaign. (2014). *Restorative practices: Fostering healthy relationships and promoting positive discipline in schools.* Accessed at http://schottfoundation.org/sites/default/files /restorative-practices-guide.pdf on September 7, 2016.

Alaska Staff Development Network. (n.d.). *Alaska administrator coaching project.* Accessed at www.asdn .org/alaska-administrator-coaching-project/2009 on October 16, 2016.

American Association of School Administrators. (2002). *Using data to improve schools: What's working.* Arlington, VA: Author. Accessed at http://aasa.org/uploadedFiles/Policy_and_Advocacy/files /UsingDataToImproveSchools.pdf on October 16, 2016.

Barton, P. E. (2003). *Parsing the achievement gap: Baselines for tracking progress.* Princeton, NJ: Policy Information Center, Educational Testing Service. Accessed at www.ets.org/Media/Education _Topics/pdf/parsing.pdf on August 2, 2016.

Biography.com editors. (2016). *John D. Rockefeller biography.* Accessed at www.biography.com/people /john-d-rockefeller-20710159#synopsis on November 14, 2016.

Black, P., & Wiliam, D. (2010). Inside the black box: Raising standards through classroom assessment. *Phi Delta Kappan, 92*(1), 81–90.

Blood, P., & Thorsborne, M. (2005, March). *The challenge of culture change: embedding restorative practice in schools.* Paper presented at the sixth International Conference on Conferencing, Circles and Other Restorative Practices, Sydney, Australia.

Blum, R. W., McNeely, C., & Nonnemaker, J. (2002). Vulnerability, risk, and protection. *Journal of Adolescent Health*, 31S, 28–39.

Board of Studies, Teaching & Educational Standards NSW. (2015). *Stage 6 languages beginners syllabuses: Advice on programming and assessment.* Accessed at www.boardofstudies.nsw.edu.au/syllabus _hsc/pdf_doc/advice-prog-language-beg.pdf on September 7, 2016.

Brookhart, S. M., Moss, C. M., & Long, B. A. (2009). Promoting student ownership of learning through high-impact formative assessment practices. *Journal of MultiDisciplinary Evaluation*, *6*(12), 52–67.

Bryk, A. S., & Schneider, B. (2002). *Trust in schools: A core resource for improvement.* New York: Sage Foundation.

Carry, D. D. (October 20, 2015). *Thinking Core,* Chicago, Illinois.

Center, D. B., Deitz, S. M., & Kaufman, M. E. (1982). Student ability, task difficulty, and inappropriate classroom behavior: A study of children with behavior disorders. *Behavior Modification*, *6*(3), 355–374.

Christie, K., Thompson, B., & Whiteley, G. (2009). *Strong leaders, strong achievement.* Denver, CO: Education Commission of the States. Accessed at www.ecs.org/clearinghouse/79/23/7923.pdf on August 11, 2016.

Clark, D. C., & Clark, S. N. (1996). Better preparation of educational leaders. *Educational Researcher*, *25*(9), 18–20.

Colberg, A. (2016, May 9). Fortune 500 CEO: The one quality every leader must have. *Fortune.* Accessed at http://fortune.com/author/alan-colberg on October 4, 2016.

Collaborative for Academic, Social, and Emotional Learning. (n.d.). *What is SEL?* Accessed at www .casel.org/what-is-sel on September 7, 2016.

Confrey, J., & Krupa, E. (2010). *Curriculum design, development, and implementation in an era of Common Core State Standards.* Columbia, MO: Center for the Study of Mathematics Curriculum.

Dhiman, S. (2015). *Gandhi and leadership: New horizons in exemplary leadership.* New York: Palgrave Macmillan.

Downey, C. J., Steffy, B. E., English, F. W., Frase, L. E., & Poston, W. K. (2004). *The three-minute classroom walk-through: Changing school supervisory practice one teacher at a time.* Thousand Oaks, CA: Corwin Press.

Education World. (n.d.). *Teachers observing teachers: A professional development tool for every school.* Accessed at www.educationworld.com/a_admin/admin/admin297.shtml on August 25, 2016.

Elias, M. J., Bruene-Butler, L., Blum, L., & Schuyler, T. (1997). How to launch a social and emotional learning program. *Educational Leadership*, *54*(8), 15–19.

Ellison, W. (1935). *Train station.* [Painting]. Chicago: Art Institute of Chicago.

English, F. W. (2008). *The art of educational leadership: Balancing performance and accountability.* Thousand Oaks, CA: SAGE.

Fisher, D., & Frey, N. (2014). *Checking for understanding: Formative assessment techniques for your classroom* (2nd ed.). Alexandria, VA: Association for Supervision and Curriculum Development.

Fisher, D., & Frey, N. (2015). *Unstoppable learning: Seven essential elements to unleash student potential.* Bloomington, IN: Solution Tree Press.

Fox, E. (2009). The role of reader characteristics in processing and learning from informational text. *Review of Educational Research*, *79*(1), 197-261.

Frey, N., & Fisher, D. (2009). The release of learning. *Principal Leadership*, *9*(6), 18–22.

Frymier, A. B., & Shulman, G. M. (1995). "What's in it for me?": Increasing content relevance to enhance students' motivation. *Communication Education, 44*(1), 40–50.

Glickman, C. D. (2002). *Leadership for learning: How to help teachers succeed.* Alexandria, VA: Association for Supervision and Curriculum Development.

Grogan, M., & Andrews, R. (2002). Defining preparation and professional development for the future. *Educational Administration Quarterly, 38*(2), 233–256.

Guskey, T. R. (2011). Five obstacles to grading reform. *Educational Leadership, 69*(3), 16–21.

Hardin, C. J. (2008). *Effective classroom management: Models and strategies for today's classrooms* (2nd ed.). Upper Saddle River, NJ: Pearson.

Hattie, J., & Timperley, H. (2007). The power of feedback. *Review of Educational Research, 77*(1), 81–112.

Heflebower, T., Hoegh, J. K., & Warrick, P. (2014). *A school leader's guide to standards-based grading.* Bloomington, IN: Marzano Research.

Hord, S. M., & Sommers, W. A. (2008). *Leading professional learning communities: Voices from research and practice.* Thousand Oaks, CA: Corwin Press.

Houston, P. D., Blankstein, A. M., & Cole, R. W. (2010). *Leadership for family and community involvement.* Thousand Oaks, CA: Corwin Press.

Huebner, T. (2010). Differentiated learning. *Educational Leadership, 67*(5), 79–81.

Hughes, L. (1949). *One-way ticket.* New York: Knopf.

Kohn, A. (2011). *The case against grades.* Accessed at www.alfiekohn.org/article/case-grades on August 25, 2016.

Larmer, J. (2015, July 13). *Project-based learning vs. problem-based learning vs. X-BL* [Blog post]. Accessed at www.edutopia.org/blog/pbl-vs-pbl-vs-xbl-john-larmer on August 12, 2016.

Leithwood, K., Louis, K. S., Anderson, S., & Wahlstrom, K. (2004). *Review of research: How leadership influences student learning.* Minneapolis: University of Minnesota, Center for Applied Research and Educational Improvement. Accessed at www.wallacefoundation.org/knowledge-center /Documents/How-Leadership-Influences-Student-Learning.pdf on October 16, 2016.

Manna, P. (2015). *Developing excellent school principals to advance teaching and learning: Considerations for state policy.* New York: Wallace Foundation.

Martin, A. J., & Dowson, M. (2009). Interpersonal relationships, motivation, engagement, and achievement: Yields for theory, current issues, and educational practice. *Review of Educational Research, 79*(1), 327–365.

Marzano, R., & Marzano, J. (2003). The key to classroom management. *Educational Leadership, 61*(1), 6–13.

McCluskey, G., Lloyd, G., Kane, J., Riddell, S., Stead, J., & Weedon, E. (2008). Can restorative practices in schools make a difference? *Educational Review, 60*(4), 405–417.

McTighe, J., & Wiggins, G. (2013). *Essential questions: Opening doors to student understanding.* Alexandria, VA: Association for Supervision and Curriculum Development.

Merrill, C. (1990). *A seed is a promise.* New York: Scholastic.

Morrison, B., Blood, P., & Thorsborne, M. (2005). Practicing restorative justice in school communities: Addressing the challenge of culture change. *Public Organization Review, 5*(4), 335–357.

Moss, C. M., & Brookhart, S. M. (2009). *Advancing formative assessment in every classroom: A guide for the instructional leader.* Alexandria, VA: Association for Supervision and Curriculum Development.

National Capitol Language Resource Center. (n.d.). *Assessing learning: Alternative assessment.* Accessed at www.nclrc.org/essentials/assessing/alternative.htm on August 25, 2016.

National Governors Association Center for Best Practices & Council of Chief State School Officers. (2010). *Common Core State Standards for English language arts and literacy in history/social studies, science, and technical subjects.* Washington, DC: Authors. Accessed at www.corestandards.org /assets/CCSSI_ELA%20Standards.pdf on August 25, 2016.

Nystrand, M. (2006). Research on the role of classroom discourse as it affects reading comprehension. *Research in the Teaching of English, 40*(4), 392–412.

Opitz, M. F. (1998). *Flexible grouping in reading: Practical ways to help all students become better readers.* New York: Scholastic.

Parsons, S. A., Dodman, S. L., & Burrowbridge, S. C. (2013). Broadening the view of differentiated instruction. *Phi Delta Kappan, 95*(1), 38–42.

Pearson, P. D., & Gallagher, M. C. (1983). The instruction of reading comprehension. *Contemporary Educational Psychology, 8*(3), 317–344.

Posner, G. J., & Rudnitsky, A. N. (1986). *Course design: A guide to curriculum development for teachers.* New York: Longman.

Posner, M. I. (1994). Attention: The mechanism of consciousness. *Proceedings of the National Academy of Sciences of the United States of America, 91*(16), 7,398–7,403.

Reddan, J., Wahlstrom, K., & Reicks, M. (2002). Children's perceived benefits and barriers in relation to eating breakfast in schools with or without universal school breakfast. *Journal of Nutrition Education and Behavior, 34*(1), 47–52.

Redford, R. (Executive producer). (2014, March 8). *Chicagoland: The fight over closing schools* [Television broadcast]. Atlanta, GA: Cable News Network.

Reeves, D. B. (2004). The case against the zero. *Phi Delta Kappan, 86*(4), 324–325.

Reeves, D. B. (2008). Effective grading practices. *Educational Leadership, 65*(5), 85–87.

Roberson, R. (2013). *Helping students find relevance.* Accessed at www.apa.org/ed/precollege/ptn /2013/09/students-relevance.aspx on August 11, 2016.

Ryan, R. M., & Deci, E. L. (2000). Intrinsic and extrinsic motivations: Classic definitions and new directions. *Contemporary Educational Psychology, 25*(1), 54–67.

Sadler, D. R. (1989). Formative assessment and the design of instructional systems. *Instructional Science, 18*(2), 119–144.

Sadler, D. R. (1998). Formative assessment: Revisiting the territory. *Assessment in Education: Principles, Policy and Practice, 5*(1), 77–84.

Seidel, T., Rimmele, R., & Prenzel, M. (2005). Clarity and coherence of lesson goals as a scaffold for student learning. *Learning and Instruction*, *15*(6), 539–556.

Selznick, P. (1984). *Leadership in administration: A sociological interpretation.* Oakland: University of California Press.

Sousa, D. A. (Ed.). (2010). *Mind, brain, and education*: *Neuroscience implications for the classroom.* Bloomington, IN: Solution Tree Press.

Stiggins, R. J., Arter, J. A., Chappuis, J., & Chappuis, S. (2007). *Classroom assessment for student learning: Doing it right—Using it well* (Special ed.). Upper Saddle River, NJ: Pearson.

Stoll, L., Fink, D., & Earl, L. (2003). *It's about learning (and it's about time).* London: Routledge.

Tieso, C. (2005). The effects of grouping practices and curricular adjustments on achievement. *Journal for the Education of the Gifted*, *29*(1), 60–89.

Tomlinson, C. A. (1999). Mapping a route toward differentiated instruction. *Educational Leadership*, *57*(1), 12–16.

Tyner, B. (2003). *Small-group reading instruction: A differentiated teaching model for beginning and struggling readers.* Newark, DE: International Reading Association.

van Veen, K., Zwart, R., & Meirink, J. (2012). What makes teacher professional development effective? A literature review. In M. Kooy & K. van Veen (Eds.), *Teacher learning that matters: International perspectives* (pp. 3–21). New York: Routledge.

Wiggins, G., & McTighe, J. (2005). *Understanding by design* (Expanded 2nd ed.). Alexandria, VA: Association for Supervision and Curriculum Development.

Index

Unstoppable Learning
Douglas Fisher and Nancy Frey
Discover proven methods to enhance teaching and learning schoolwide. Identify questions educators should ask to guarantee a positive classroom culture where students learn from each other, not just teachers. Explore ways to adapt teaching in response to students' individual needs.
BKF662

From Leading to Succeeding
Douglas Reeves
Utilizing the crucial elements of effective leadership—purpose, trust, focus, leverage, feedback, change, and sustainability—education leaders can overcome any challenge. This book confronts leadership myths, offers guidance on best leadership practices, and provides the support leaders need to succeed.
BKF649

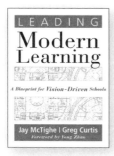

Leading Modern Learning
Jay McTighe and Greg Curtis
Bring focus to your mission for modern learning. Explore the building blocks for creating a curriculum that supports modern learning, an assessment system that captures evidence of 21st century skills, and instruction that aligns with modern learning principles.
BKF551

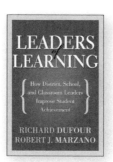

Leaders of Learning
Richard DuFour and Robert J. Marzano
Together, the authors focus on district leadership, principal leadership, and team leadership and address how individual teachers can be most effective in leading students—by learning with colleagues how to implement the most promising pedagogy in their classrooms.
BKF455

Wait! Your professional development journey doesn't have to end with the last pages of this book.

We realize improving student learning doesn't happen overnight. And your school or district shouldn't be left to puzzle out all the details of this process alone.

No matter where you are on the journey, we're committed to helping you get to the next stage.

Take advantage of everything from **custom workshops** to **keynote presentations** and **interactive web and video conferencing**. We can even help you develop an action plan tailored to fit your specific needs.

Let's get the conversation started.

Call 888.763.9045 today.

SolutionTree.com